KARL BARTH'S TABLE TALK

KARL BARTH'S TABLE TALK

Recorded and Edited by
JOHN D. GODSEY

JOHN KNOX PRESS
RICHMOND, VIRGINIA

Published in Great Britain by Oliver & Boyd, Ltd.,
Edinburgh and London, and in the United States of
America by John Knox Press, Richmond, Virginia

Library of Congress Catalog Card Number: 63-20140

Dedicated to
FRAÜLEIN CHARLOTTE VON KIRSCHBAUM
*the devoted helper of Professor Barth
and his students*

CONTENTS

	PAGE
FOREWORD	vii
PART I: AN INTRODUCTION TO KARL BARTH's *Church Dogmatics*	I
A. The Architecture of Karl Barth's *Church Dogmatics* (by John D. Godsey)	7
B. Question and Answer Period	12
PART II: CONCERNING KARL BARTH's *Church Dogmatics* VOLUME I: 'THE DOCTRINE OF THE WORD OF GOD'	19
PART III: CONCERNING SEVERAL OF KARL BARTH's MONOGRAPHS	70
A. *Church and State*	70
B. *The Christian Community and the Civil Community*	77
C. *The Teaching of the Church Regarding Baptism*	85
D. *The Christian Understanding of Revelation*	92
APPENDIX: OUTLINE OF KARL BARTH's *Church Dogmatics*	100

FOREWORD

For many years theological students from the Anglo-Saxon world made the trek to Basel, Switzerland, to sit at the feet of Professor Karl Barth. For most, the major barrier to fruitful communication proved to be the German language, and it was to overcome this formidable obstacle that Professor Barth instituted about mid-century a biweekly 'English-speaking Colloquium'. Every other Tuesday evening those students whose mother tongue is English were invited to the Professor's home on Pilgerstrasse, where they would sit around the dining-room table and discuss theology in this intimate and convivial atmosphere. In a few years the increase of students necessitated a move to a seminar room in Basel University's Theological Seminar Building, which overlooks the Rhine River, and when Professor Barth changed his own residence to Bruderholzallee, he made arrangements for the Colloquium to be held henceforth in a private room at the nearby Bruderholz Restaurant. Although much of the earlier intimacy was lost, the *Gemütlichkeit* and the liveliness of theological discussion remained undiminished.

The conduct of the Colloquium was quite simple. A section from one of Professor Barth's own writings was assigned in advance for general reading, and one student assumed the task of presenting a short précis of the text, together with a few questions to stimulate dialogue. After some introductory remarks on the adequacy of the presentation, Professor Barth took up in succession each of the prepared questions, attempting to formulate answers that conveyed meaning in the language of those assembled. Queries from other members of the Colloquium were entertained from time to time. Needless to say, the quality of the questions varied according to the maturity of insight and the erudition of the questioner, and it should be remembered that the participants ranged from professors on sabbatical leave to students who were just beginning their theological studies. Also, the diversity of theological and ecclesiastical traditions represented should be kept in mind, as well as the fact that those present usually included both staunch advocates and intransigent opponents of Barth's theology.

Regardless of how astute or naïve or leading a question might have been, Professor Barth treated it sympathetically and with theological seriousness. He often struggled with the English language, delving for clarification of a question or grasping for the right expression of a theological idea, but for one who learned the language relatively late in life and mainly by reading English mystery novels, he handled this foreign medium amazingly well! Even his humour and wit came through, and the warmth and vigour of his personality were always evident.

In what follows an attempt is made to extend some of Professor Barth's Colloquia to a wider audience and thereby to provide an unusual introduction not only to an outstanding theology but also to a great man. In Part I, I have reproduced a paper of my own that was presented at the first session of the Colloquium in the fall of 1955. This represents a special assignment designed to introduce the new students to Barth's *Church Dogmatics*, and it is hoped that it will fulfil that function here. Part II presents questions and answers concerning Volume I of the *Church Dogmatics*, which has to do with 'The Doctrine of the Word of God'. All of Part 1 and a few sections of Part 2 are dealt with. Part III deals with four important monographs from the pen of Professor Barth, namely, *Church and State*, *The Christian Community and the Civil Community*, *The Teaching of the Church Regarding Baptism*, and *The Christian Understanding of Revelation*. The entire series covers a period beginning with the Winter Semester of 1953 and concluding with the Summer Semester of 1956. It should be pointed out that not all questions relate to the specified text, for it is only natural that students should take their golden opportunity to pursue questions nearest and dearest to their hearts!

The record of what took place during the various sessions of the Colloquium is taken from my own notes, and it is obvious that my note-taking was better on some occasions than on others. I can only offer sincere apologies for any incompleteness or inaccuracies. Since I was usually more concerned to record Professor Barth's comments than the questions of students, I frankly have had to reconstruct the query in some instances. No attempt has been made to distinguish among students, the letter 'S' being used throughout to designate their contributions and the letter 'B' those of Professor Barth. I wish to acknowledge my indebtedness to all those whose presentations and questions make this work possible, and to express special gratitude to Karl Barth for permitting this unguarded dialogue to be published. He of course can assume only limited liability for the contents, since the work does not presume to be his *ipsissima verba*, but he has read the manuscript and found it 'interesting and amusing'.

JOHN D. GODSEY

Drew University
Madison, New Jersey
February 1962

PART I

An Introduction to Karl Barth's Church Dogmatics

A. Paper by John D. Godsey*
THE ARCHITECTURE OF KARL BARTH'S *Church Dogmatics*

INTRODUCTION

IT may sound presumptuous to speak of the architecture of a
dogmatics which is not yet complete, but the size and scope
of Professor Barth's *Church Dogmatics* to date would seem to
justify our attempt to examine its outer structure in order to
discover the basic dynamic principles involved in this Protestant
'Summa'. In following this procedure, however, we should be
aware that we are working backwards, for, unlike the many
dogmatics in which the Christian faith has been forced into a
pre-established mould, Professor Barth has been willing to cast
the mould in accordance with the demands of the faith itself.
This is not to deny in any way the obvious human element
involving meticulous planning and unusually sensitive organisational skill, but is to state clearly that the *Church Dogmatics* is not
a system conforming to the dictates of human reason, but is a
bold yet humble attempt to write a systematic theology that
conforms to the revelation of God in Jesus Christ. As such, the
architectural plans must necessarily result from obedient and
faithful listening to the Word of God spoken to the Church, and
all future designs must remain fluid and prepared for unex-
pected changes.

Anyone who has investigated the growth of the *Church
Dogmatics* since its inception in 1932 will soon discover that the
author's well-laid plans have often been altered by the hard
demands of the Word of God. To be sure, after publishing his
first *Prolegomena to Dogmatics* in 1927 and then experiencing the
necessity of completely rewriting the very same *Prolegomena*
during the next eleven years, Professor Barth had firmly established the five doctrines that constitute the main divisions of his

* This paper, in slightly altered form, was read before Barth's Colloquium on
8th November 1955 and published in the *Scottish Journal of Theology*, Vol. 9, No. 3,
pp. 236-50.

Dogmatics. But if one reads the projected outline for the future course of the *Dogmatics* which is given at the end of Volume I, Part 2, one will be struck by the structural changes that have subsequently occurred. A more recent attempt at prognostication, namely, the projected outline for the Doctrine of Reconciliation that stands at the beginning of Volume IV, Part 1, has already proved unreliable in some details.

Keeping this living character in mind, our task is now to consider the structure of the *Church Dogmatics* as it stands before us and to attempt to discover why it is so constructed.

1. *General Observations*

Let us begin with some general observations that even a casual reader should discover. First, the title of *Church Dogmatics* is to be taken seriously. From the outset this theology is bound to the *sphere of the Church* and is only understandable and meaningful within its borders. It arose from a pastoral concern that prompted a man to dare to be the Church in his own concrete situation by attempting to carry out the function of dogmatics within the Church, that is, by measuring the present proclamation of the Church according to the yardstick of the essence of the Church, which is Jesus Christ as He is attested in Holy Scripture. This task which was undertaken is no auxiliary task, but an integral and necessary and continuing function of the Christian community. The seriousness with which Professor Barth takes this ecclesiological responsibility has led to a dogmatics in which the Church is not simply reflecting, but is in conversation with itself. The reader is immediately impressed by the number of excursuses in which both the prominent and the obscure theological voices from all periods of Church history are allowed to make their pertinent contributions to today's conversation—an architectural feature which, indeed, has added considerably to the length of the *Dogmatics*.

A second general feature is the important role that *biblical exegesis* plays in the structure of the *Church Dogmatics*. This can easily be detected by the great number of excursuses that are devoted to the exegetical bases for dogmatic statements about the faith. This stems from Professor Barth's conviction that the Bible, which is the book of the Church that contains the witness of the prophets and apostles to God's self-revelation in Christ, must be considered in utmost seriousness as the criterion for judging Church proclamation. The dogmatician must always be engaged in the task of biblical exegesis, and the exegesis must ever lead back to dogmatics.

A further characteristic, which is obvious to anyone who so much as peruses the table of contents, is the *incorporation of ethics* as an integral part of the *Church Dogmatics*. This unusual procedure follows from the author's belief that Christian ethics is no more and no less than the Doctrine of the Command of God (as event) and therefore cannot stand isolated from the realm of dogmatics in the Church. Accordingly, there is a discussion of general ethics at the close of the Doctrine of God and a discussion of special ethics at the close of the Doctrines of Creation, Reconciliation, and Redemption.

Finally, a fourth characteristic, which is immediately apparent, is the *Trinitarian* structure of the *Church Dogmatics*. Here we do not find the Loci-scheme of Melanchthon and most old orthodox dogmatics or the credal formulation of Calvin or the inductive logic of Schleiermacher, but a willingness to follow the structural lines of the revelation itself. That is, the architecture bears the impress of God's revelation to His Church in the Lord Jesus Christ, a revelation that demands the ultimate formulation of a Doctrine of the Trinity, because the Doctrine of the Trinity is the great methodological interpretation of God's revelation. We might also describe the architecture as 'revelational' or 'Christocentric', but each of these designations would have to be qualified and interpreted in terms of the Trinity, since the Doctrines of Perichoresis (that God's three modes of existence mutually penetrate each other or 'inexist') and Appropriations (that a special word or deed is attributed to this or that Person of the Godhead) and the rule *opera trinitatis ad extra sunt indivisa* are basic to Christian thinking about God. Thus the 'revelation', which is 'Christocentric', is simply the revelation of the triune God: the Father, the Son, the Holy Spirit. From this perspective we can appreciate the division of the *Church Dogmatics* into its five main parts: (1) the Doctrine of the Word of God, which investigates the basis for the revelation of the triune God; (2) the Doctrine of God, which deals with the knowledge and reality of the one God who reveals Himself in threeness; (3) the Doctrine of Creation, which concerns the activity appropriated to God the Father; (4) the Doctrine of Reconciliation, the activity appropriated to God the Son; (5) the Doctrine of Redemption, the activity appropriated to God the Holy Spirit.

2. *Specific Observations*

(a) *The Doctrine of the Word of God*

Now let us turn our attention to some of the interesting details of the architecture of the *Church Dogmatics*. First of all, we discover that in the Doctrine of the Word of God we are dealing with '*prolegomena*' to dogmatics. This is no accident, because Professor Barth believes that dogmatics must first forge its own epistemological tools and thus render an account of its own special pathway to knowledge before it can proceed to its main task. *Prolegomena* are not intended to give the revelation in Christ a natural substructure that would more or less justify it before the court of human reason, that is, an apologetic opportunity to prove or defend the faith of those on the outside, but are an inner necessity grounded in the paradoxical fact of heresy within the Church itself. Here the two heresies that are opposed throughout the *Church Dogmatics* come to light: pietistic-rationalistic Modernism, which finds its point of departure for dogmatic statements in a general understanding of man, his world or his existence, and Roman Catholicism, which begins with the existence of a Church in which Jesus Christ is no longer its free Lord, but is bound up with the existence of the Church itself.

A closer examination of the contents of the *Prolegomena* will divulge that Professor Barth begins with the Word of God, that is, with God in His concrete revelatory action in the event of Jesus Christ, who *is* the Word of God. In other words, the architecture shows us that we begin with God and not man, with the reality of revelation and not its possibility. The special way of knowledge of the Christian faith, then, is not grounded in any capacity or possibility of man, but in God's own sovereign freedom. Man can know God only because God makes Himself known to man—this is the *petitio principii* of which the author of the *Church Dogmatics* is not ashamed. The whole volume is really a commentary on the one sentence: God reveals Himself as Lord.

Now that the Word of God is established as the criterion of

4

dogmatics, the structure of the remainder of the *Prolegomena* is simply an exposition of the threefold form of this one Word of God, which, according to Professor Barth, is the only admissible analogy for the Trinity. Chapter 2 deals with the 'revealed Word' or 'Revelation of God', Chapter 3 with the 'written Word' or 'Holy Scripture', Chapter 4 with the 'preached Word' or 'Church Proclamation'. What can we learn here? First, the order is important. Unlike most Protestant dogmatics, we do not begin with the doctrine of Holy Scripture, but with the Incarnation itself. Here we see that the 'revealed Word', which *has happened* once and for all time in the historical event of Jesus Christ, must be given a prior and determinative position above and beyond the 'written Word' and 'the preached Word', which must ever again *become* God's Word. Thus the Bible can never become a 'paper pope', but retains its basic character as witness. Second, we should note well that there is no room left for a natural theology. This does not mean that there is no natural knowledge of God, but it means that apart from God's own self-revelation man has no knowledge that can be appealed to as a basis for the knowledge of God that he has in Christ. A natural theology, therefore, has no real theological significance and deserves no place in the dogmatics of the Church.

(b) The Doctrine of God

Next we examine the Doctrine of God, which purposely *follows* the exposition of the Doctrine of the Trinity, a reversal of the usual procedure in dogmatics. What is the reason for this architectural feature? Just this: by previously establishing the Doctrine of the Trinity as a functional and not a metaphysical doctrine, that is, God in action and not in static being, Professor Barth is now able to avoid the usual speculative and fruitless discussion of the ontology of the Trinity and the abstract attributes of God's being. Here we see at work the basic insight that Christian thinking about God must move from action to ontology, from the economic Trinity to the ontological Trinity, never *vice versa*. There is no possible retreat from the *Deus revelatus* to a *Deus absconditus*, no going behind God's own revelation of Himself in Jesus Christ. God is antecedently in Himself exactly the same God He reveals Himself to be in His acting in history. The mystery of God is preserved precisely in His revelation, in the Incarnation of the Word.

Chapters 5 and 6, which deal with the Knowledge and Reality of God, reveal that the certainty and actuality of the revelation are axiomatic for theological thinking. No one acquainted with Professor Barth's theology should be surprised that the question of the existence of God is never raised. Instead, it is simply affirmed that the triune God exists as the One who freely loves, and His perfections—the term that the author prefers to that of 'attributes'—are those of the divine loving (here are coupled in the most surprising way grace and holiness, mercy and righteousness, patience and wisdom) and those of the divine freedom (no less surprising is the coupling here of unity and omnipresence, constancy and omnipotence, eternity and glory). All of this points back to the basic primacy of the revelation and to the fact that God's being is understood properly solely from God's action.

In Chapter 7 we come to an architectural positioning of decisive importance within the *Church Dogmatics*. At the very heart of the Doctrine of God we find a discussion of what Professor Barth asserts to be the heart of the Gospel: the Doctrine of God's Gracious Election. Election is for the Doctrine of God what the Doctrine of Reconciliation is for the whole of the *Church Dogmatics*: its heart and centre and foundation, upon which everything else depends. Election means reconciliation. Thus it is not abstractly grounded in the usual omnipotence of God, but in Jesus Christ Himself, the gracious revelation of God's love. It is also not placed as a peripheral dogmatic concern, as a catch-all doctrine that takes care of everything beyond man's comprehension; it is made as central as the Gospel, which it itself is. Election is not some hidden and horrible decree, but the decree revealed in Jesus Christ, who is the electing God and the elected man. It is important to note that the structure here follows a particular order: the election of Jesus Christ, the election of the community, the election of the individual. This again points to the importance and function of the Church, which is ever in the foreground of the author's thought. But what about reprobation? This receives no section of its own in the architecture, for even non-election is known only in the election of Jesus Christ. In Him God reveals a double predestination, that is, an eternal will that contains a Yes and a No, but in the election of Jesus Christ God has intended the Yes for man and the No for Himself. God

6

Himself has chosen our rejection. From this follows the basic thought that evil is simply a power that has been overthrown and condemned to impotency, that Satan is not God's ultimately real adversary. All of this is not to infer a doctrine of *apokatastasis* (universal salvation), however, but asserts that the Bible knows no ultimate dualism, but the supremacy of God's grace and the impotence of human wickedness in the face of it.

Directly following the Doctrine of God's Gracious Election, we have in Chapter 8 a discussion of God's Command. This is by no means an accident. Election and command belong inextricably together and must be viewed in that order. The correspondence to Professor Barth's famous coupling of 'Gospel and Law' over against the Lutheran 'Law and Gospel' is obvious. The two are to be differentiated, but never separated, and Law is always to be seen in the light of the Gospel. In Christian theological thinking it is of critical importance that we always move from Gospel to Law, just as we must go from justification to sanctification, from faith to works, from Church to State. In other words, here we have a Christological concept of the Law that excludes any foundation in natural law or orders of creation: God's *Nomos* and God's *Logos* are ultimately identical, for Law is the form of the Gospel. There is no Law and no Gospel in and for themselves, but only the one Word of God. This means that God's command is an event, not a general proposition. In our context it also means that the concrete form of election is sanctification. Jesus Christ is the sanctifying God and the sanctified man.

(c) *The Doctrine of Creation*

The Doctrine of Creation can properly come only *after* the Doctrine of God, the heart of which is God's Gracious Election. This structural arrangement signifies Professor Barth's conviction that God is not known first of all in His creation, but in the revelation of his Lordship in Jesus Christ. Only from the prior viewpoint of God's election or reconciliation, that is, only for the eyes of faith, does the world become a creation instead of a cosmos, does nature take on glory. From this supposition it is not surprising that the author discusses at the very beginning the relation between creation and covenant. The connexion is integral. The covenant of grace, which is concretely actualised in the history of salvation, is the inner meaning and determinative factor of all history. The first creation saga (Genesis 1-2.4a) affirms that creation is the external basis of the covenant, whereas the second saga (Genesis 2.4b-3) discloses the covenant as the internal basis of the creation.

After establishing this crucial starting-point, which might be termed a Christological supposition or, seen from man's side, a supposition of faith, we can now understand in some measure the unique way in which Professor Barth handles the Doctrine of Creation. Since knowledge of creation stems only from the revelation of God in Christ, creation can only be conceived in terms of an analogy, the most inclusive term for this being *analogia fidei* (analogy of faith), that is, an analogy that is erected by the choice and decision of God Himself in His free grace and is only visible for faith. Here we see a powerful turning against Roman Catholicism's *analogia entis* (analogy of being), which subsumes both Creator and creature under the higher category of 'being', and Modernism's various world views, which subordinate revelation to reason. Here we meet the consequences of the rejection of natural theology. From this perspective Professor Barth is now able to speak about creaturely history in terms of an analogy or correspondence to the history of the covenant; of God's creature in terms of an *analogia relationis*, that is, of an analogy between the I and Thou in God Himself and the fact that the creature is created as man and woman (this communal relation is the *Imago Dei*, which is not lost in the Fall, but which first becomes understandable in the light of the relation between Jesus Christ and His Church); of the command of God the Creator, which is not founded on independent orders of creation, but is related solely to the real ground of creation, Jesus Christ.

What further can we learn from the architecture of the Doctrine of Creation? First, we may note an omission. There is no doctrine of the original state of man before the Fall—what is usually called the state of perfection or original righteousness. The fact that this doctrine is left out of the *Church Dogmatics* stems from the author's belief that the Bible teaches us nothing theologically significant about a so-called *Uroffenbarung*, that we can know only of man as sinner—and this from the revelation in Christ. Second, the relatively little space devoted to the 'Nothingness' (*das Nichtige*), which encompasses the concepts of chaos, fallen creation, cosmic evil, demonology, and so forth, is noteworthy. This does not signify that the Nothingness is not taken seriously, but emphasises the fact that Professor Barth sees in the Bible absolutely no dualism, no splitting up of reality into two conflicting, balanced principles. The Nothingness belongs to the sphere of God's No, to the negation of grace, to what God has rejected. The 'chaos' of Genesis 1.2, for instance, is not some primal stuff that existed before creation, but is simply the possibility that God scornfully passed over. The Nothingness, therefore, does not exist as God and the creature exist, but in a way peculiar to itself and known only to God, because it is grounded in His negation. Only in Jesus Christ do we understand the Nothingness: the Incarnation reveals that the Nothingness exists, and the Crucifixion and Resurrection reveal that it exists improperly and must pass away. Third, from the structure of the Doctrine of Creation we can observe the large share of attention given to the creature and the relatively small amount devoted to the so-called world of nature. The stated reason for this is that the Word of God gives an ontology of man, but not an ontology of heaven and earth. Thus there is no biblical world view or biblical cosmology, whereas there is a definite biblical anthropology. Last, but not least, it is interesting to observe that Professor Barth has not hesitated to deal fully with the subject of the Angels, which he discusses more from the viewpoint of their service than their nature.

(d) The Doctrine of Reconciliation

We now turn our attention to the structural and material centre of the *Church Dogmatics*: the crucial and pivotal Doctrine of Reconciliation. This doctrine stands in the middle between the Doctrines of Creation and Redemption and forms the proper link between them. Since the covenant is the presupposition of reconciliation, the Doctrine of Reconciliation naturally *follows* the Doctrine of Creation. In the event of reconciliation Jesus Christ, 'God with us', fulfils the broken covenant, thus making possible man's eschatological redemption. Therefore the Doctrine of Reconciliation naturally *precedes* the Doctrine of Redemption.

In Chapter 13 we find a synopsis of the unusually beautiful structure of the Doctrine of Reconciliation. Here Christ's working Person or personal Work in the total of the happening of reconciliation is viewed under three Christological aspects in three chapters constructed in exact parallel. Chapter 14 deals with the knowledge of Jesus Christ, who is the true, namely, the self-humiliating and thus the reconciling, God: what the old dogmatics called Christ's priestly office. Chapter 15 deals with the knowledge of Jesus Christ, who is the true, namely the exalted-by-God and thus the reconciled, man: Christ's kingly office. Chapter 16 deals with the knowledge of Jesus Christ the Mediator, who, as the concrete unity of God and man, is the Guarantor and Witness of our atonement: Christ's prophetic office. Each of the three chapters has five paragraphs, the first of which is a discussion of the Christological aspects just outlined. This is followed by a paragraph dealing with the forms of human sin, respectively, man's pride, sloth, and falsehood; next a paragraph on what objectively takes place in the event of reconciliation: man's justification, sanctification, and calling; then a paragraph on the subjective realisation of reconciliation through the work of the Holy Spirit in the gathering, upbuilding, and sending of the Christian community; and a final paragraph on the being of Christians in Jesus Christ in faith, in love, and in hope. The Doctrine of Reconciliation closes with another chapter on special ethics, in which the Command of God is considered from the viewpoint of Law.

What can we learn from the architectural plans of this doctrine? First, we should notice that Professor Barth does not deal with independent Doctrines of Christology, Soteriology, and Ecclesiology, does not investigate separately the Doctrines of the Person and the Work of Christ, as in classical Christology. To do so is to divide what can be seen properly only as a whole: Jesus Christ existing in the totality of His work as Reconciler. The existence of Jesus Christ as true God, as true man, and the unity of both (God-man) is only understood from the completed act of the reconciliation of man with God in history. Once again we see the consequences of the principle that being must be understood in the light of action. Second, it is obvious that the doctrine of the two 'Natures' of Christ (His divinity and His humanity) and the doctrine of the two 'States' of Christ (His humiliation and His exaltation) have been related to each other in a fresh and unusual way. Consciously deviating from the old Protestant dogmatics, Professor Barth endeavours to interpret the two States of Christ not as states that follow one another, but as two sides or directions or forms of the one material, reconciling act of Jesus Christ; to interpret the Doctrine of the two States from that of the two Natures, and *vice versa*; and to emphasise that in all this we have to do with the one God graciously and sovereignly acting as the One who freely loves.

Third, we should note that the author has given precedence to what the old dogmaticians designated Christ's high-priestly office over His kingly office, because he feels that it is more precise and also more comprehensive. Fourth, it is noteworthy that no independent Doctrine of Sin, which in most dogmatics occupies a space between the Doctrine of Creation and the Doctrine of Reconciliation, is to be found in the *Church Dogmatics*. Instead, sin is discussed *after* Christology as an integral part of the total Doctrine of Reconciliation, an arrangement that derives from the conviction that sin is only understandable in the light of the Gospel. Fifth, Christ's objective accomplishment of reconciliation for man is clearly distinguished from man's subjective appropriation of the same. This is necessary, because the latter concerns the being and work of the Holy Spirit.

Sixth, it is important to observe that Professor Barth gives priority to the question about Christendom over the question about the individual Christian when he handles the problem of the subjective realisation of grace. This again emphasises the fact that the reconciling work of Christ is appropriated by the individual only through his participation in Christ's earthly-historical form of existence, the Church. By holding to this order the author is able to avoid any tendency toward the rank individualism that has continually plagued Protestantism. Seventh, we should be aware that no discussion of the doctrine of the Sacraments—of Baptism and the Lord's Supper—is to be found in the major parts of the Doctrine of Reconciliation proper; these will be considered in the context of the chapter on special ethics at the close of the doctrine. The reason for this important change in the architectural plans will have to await a fuller explanation by Professor Barth himself. For now we can only speculate that it is in accordance with the fact that he hardly uses the general concept of 'sacrament' any more. Finally, in his paragraphs on the Christian life in Christ the author has deviated from St. Paul's classical order of faith, hope, and love, changing the order to faith, love, and hope. We can only ponder whether this is merely a matter of organisational tactics, since 'hope' would quite naturally lead to the Doctrine of the 'Last Things', or whether it has real theological significance.

(e) The Doctrine of Redemption

The final volume of the *Church Dogmatics* will undertake an elaboration of the Doctrine of Redemption, that is, of the activity of God that is properly appropriated to His mode of existence as Holy Spirit. It may be a surprise to some readers that man's 'redemption' is directly connected to the Holy Spirit rather than the Son. That this is theologically correct, however, has already been grounded exegetically in Volume I, Part 1. In this final section Professor Barth must discuss the Doctrine of the 'Last Things', of the Final Judgment and Consummation, of the Command of God from the viewpoint of Promise. We may expect that the Christological thread will be traced to the final page of the *Church Dogmatics*, that Jesus Christ, who is the Alpha, will also be the Omega!

B. Question and Answer Period

Barth's comments on the paper: Very good, but perhaps you have been more consistent than the work itself! I see more complexities—even contradictions!—in the *Church Dogmatics*. However, the main lines are certainly correct. It would be good to publish your paper in America, where so many misunderstand my theology.

S: Do you see any danger of the *Church Dogmatics* becoming for Protestantism what Thomas Aquinas' *Summa Theologica* is for Roman Catholicism, that is, leading to a period of repristination in which the Church's continuing function of writing dogmatics is neglected?

B: Yes, there is a danger—an honourable danger to be compared to Aquinas! Thank you! After Aquinas there was much repeating of his theology. Even Aquinas repeated a great deal from the *Sentences* of Peter Lombard, who erected the great 'system' of the Middle Ages. In fact, all theologians did until Calvin. Yes, a danger could arise; future theologians might be tempted to fall back on a scholasticism of this kind. You are not the first to ask me if all is not said here in my dogmatics. No, no, no! The Church's *continuing* function of writing dogmatics cannot be relinquished! A living Church will have a living dogmatics.

S: Although you have often said that it would be possible to begin a dogmatics with any of the great Christian doctrines, do you really believe you could begin the *Church Dogmatics* with any other doctrine than that of the Trinity? After examining the architecture, I am doubtful!

B: Christian truth is a living whole. I do not like the term 'architecture' too much, for it connotes 'building' or 'system'. Christian truth is like a globe, where every point points to the centre. We must hold out the possibility of beginning a dogmatics with any doctrine, for instance, with the doctrine of the Church, or with the topic in Calvin's Book III: sanctification, or even a universal doctrine of the Holy Spirit. Indeed, we might even begin with the Christian man! The Christian and the Christian theologian must be a *free* man. I opposed Schleiermacher and subjectivism because it was necessary at the time. Another time, those who have learned something from the *Church Dogmatics* may perhaps begin with Christian subjectivism. Why not? Of course, freedom means responsibility and obedience, it is true. But freedom means real freedom! Remember what I recently said in my lectures: '*Methodus est arbitraria*'; procedures may change. In this time I begin with the Doctrine of the Trinity. In another time theology and its situation will change. I am interested with a passion in the freedom of theology, and I must be interested in the freedom of future theologians from the *Church Dogmatics*. Only then am I rightly understood! I began with the Trinity. But I can imagine even Schleiermacher's procedure, that is, *ending* with the Trinity, being correct.

S: But could you begin anywhere but with the *Prolegomena*?

B: It would be possible to make the questions of *prolegomena* into a *postlegomena*. Methodology and epistemology could come at the end of the dogmatics—or even in the middle. Why not? I have chosen the most simple way. I can imagine a more spiritual procedure. Perhaps I am too much of a schoolmaster in this work. Another generation may say, 'Let's begin at the beginning!' From heaven I shall look down, speculate, and not be opposed.

S: Even if they start with 'existence'?

B: Please! Only with the existence of man in the communion

of the Holy Spirit. Not everything is allowed! We cannot begin with Bultmann's starting-point: man's existence as such. But I can imagine a situation when all of the theologians (perhaps not all!) meet in heaven and speak together. All will refer to their books! But then they will see clearly; each will understand the other. One might say, 'Yes, dear Schleiermacher, I understand you now. You were right, except on some points!' And he will understand, and he will tell you some things about your theology! There will be agreement in the disagreement, and no more disagreement in agreement. This is more serious han you think, perhaps.

S: In your theology you always emphasise that God is antecedently in Himself what He reveals Himself to be in Jesus Christ, that God is free from us as well as free for us. What is he Christological reason for this 'extra nos' in a Church whose sole knowledge is of a God who is 'pro nobis' in Jesus Christ?

B: The Christological reason for this can only be understood in terms of the Doctrine of Election: God's Gracious Election. If that is so, if reconciliation is based on the free, gracious election of God, then we must accept in the living God no external necessity. He wills and acts, but always in freedom. He is what He reveals Himself to be in Christ, but exactly there He reveals Himself as the God of free grace. God is not bound to the world. He binds Himself! The covenant is His eternal will, but His *free* will. Even in the ontological realm there is an *extra nos*. In the sense that we are not God, that God is God and we are only His creatures, God is *extra nos*. But as such He is not only free to do without us, but He is loving in His freedom. In His love He will not remain *extra nos*! He begins His work with us from eternity. There is no contradiction between God's being *extra nos* and His action for us.

S: Is there a separation between Word and existence?

B: Yes, in the sense that Word is event. God *speaks* His Word to us. That is, the Word is not identical with our existence, but addresses us. There is a meeting of the two: God and us, each existing. The Word becomes flesh, enters our world, in faith even becomes our 'possession', but is not identical with us. The Word remains free.

S: If Jesus Christ is the only 'real' man for God and we are only real men in so far as we are 'in Christ', which you interpret to mean 'in the Church', and if the Church is an event which happens from time to time when the proclamation of the Church becomes the Word of God, then how do you give ontological significance to your anthropology? Wherein does the continuity lie, since being infers continuity?

B: Have I said that Christ is the only real man?

S: Yes, in Volume III, Part 2, you have a section on 'Jesus Christ, *the* man for God'.

B: Oh ho! Now I know what you mean. Jesus Christ is the only real man for God. Everything depends on what we mean by 'real'. Here I do not mean that we men do not *exist*, but that there is a kind of existing that lacks reality. Man in sin exists, but is not 'real reality'. He does not accomplish what it means to be a man. Yes, Christ is the only real man before God. He fulfils the real existence of man. We do not. We have an incomplete or lost reality. My point in anthropology is that every man is a *virtual* brother of Christ, because the whole world is healed in and through Christ. Every man has his destination in Christ and is virtually His brother. Every man is living not 'in' but 'for' Christ, 'in view of' Christ. Because there is no man without Christ, no man who is not a virtual brother of Christ, we may say that there is no reality of manhood apart from Him. However, humanity does not begin only in Christ. If it begins there, it is only because man *discovers* truth, because he discovers Christ.

S: What is the ontology of man in the Bible—a being in sin?

B: Certainly *not*! As sinner man puts in question his true being. He is a being in his qualification as a creature of God, who has created the world in Christ. Even before he becomes a Christian he is in continuity with God in Christ, but he has not yet discovered it. He realises it only when he begins to believe.

S: Do you understand the 'Body of Christ' ontologically or metaphorically?

B: It is certainly a metaphor, but a very expansive one. We cannot express this truth without metaphorical language: Christ, the Head; we the Church, His Body. Not everyone is in the Body of Christ. That is clear in the New Testament. The Body is made up of called, hearing, accepting believers. But everyone is a *virtual* member of the Body. No one is excluded. That is a question of mission. Missionaries must tell people the truth about themselves. Missionaries must believe that Christ died *for them*: Indians, Chinese, Africans, and so on. The missionary approaches not an ontologically different kind of human being, but beings who are, not in the Body, but in the realm of Christ, in the power of His sovereignty. The missionary announces: 'Christ is your Lord!' 'Mine?' 'Yes, yours!' The term 'virtually' here is opposed to 'actually'. It is not wise to describe the actual existence of virtual brothers in Christ. You cannot say any more than that 'they are sinners'. However, we should not approach them as sinners, but as virtual brothers. Remember the degree to which we are all only virtual brothers! If we understand our own situation, then we will understand those *extra muros*.

S: Then there are not two ontologies: one being in sin, one being in grace?

B: No, there is only one ontology for all men.

S: Because of your desire to avoid any dualism between God and His adversaries (Satan and his angels, principalities and powers), it seems to me that you have left no room in your Doctrine of Reconciliation for what appears to be a genuine biblical element in the work of Christ, namely, His triumph over these adversaries as Christus Victor. Is this criticism valid?

B: I do not think it is a valid criticism. This sort of question can only be asked by those who cannot see the wood for the trees. If you consider the whole of the *Church Dogmatics*, including all that is said regarding sin and Satan, how could I give a stronger statement regarding Christus Victor? I am often criticised about this. Berkouwer, in his survey of my theology in his book, *The Triumph of Grace in the Theology of Karl Barth*, complains of too much triumph in the *Church Dogmatics*, because I treat demons, sin, the Nothingness, and so forth, too lightly. Now you say there is not enough room for the triumph—just the opposite! How can we make clear the victory of Christ? In this way: when speaking of sin, demons, darkness, by *not* speaking of them in too tragic a manner—like the German theologians, all so serious! The further north you go in Germany, the more they are concerned with the realm of darkness. And if you move to the Scandinavian countries, all is darkness: God against Satan, and *vice versa*! Gustaf Wingren is proud to be a 'serious' theologian, because he takes Satan seriously. I understand. But because there must be room for the victory of Christ, you cannot be so anxious and pitiful and sad. Go on, explain the Work and Word of Christ, and you are above! We cannot deny the reality of evil and the Nothingness, but in and with Christ we are above these mysteries. It is not wise to be too serious. We must be serious, of course; life is hard. But we are not to take Satan as a reality in the same sense that Jesus is real.

S: I asked the question because in your Doctrine of Reconciliation the sections dealing with what is overcome in reconciliation all begin with 'man's': *man's* pride, *man's* sloth, *man's* falsehood. Where is the place for objective evil beyond man?

B: Aha! Now I understand: the powers behind man! You are right about the titles, but if you read these sections, do you not have the impression that, without the mythology of 'powers', sin is taken seriously? You cannot speak even of powers except in terms of man's sin. Powers are really there, but the New Testament does not make a division between what happens in the world and 'powers of darkness'.

S: Calvin deals with the offices of Christ in the order: prophet, king, priest. Schleiermacher uses the order: prophet, priest, king. You use the order: priest, king, prophet. Would you explain the significance of your architectural arrangement with regard to these former dogmaticians?

B: The ordinary order for Calvin and Reformed theologians is prophet, king, priest, for Schleiermacher and Lutheran theologians: prophet, priest, king. Now you want to know why I use the order: priest, king, prophet. For me the priestly and kingly offices in the narrower sense are the doings of Christ. The humiliation of God in becoming man and the exaltation of man up to God are respectively Christ's priestly and Christ's kingly work. Christ the Prophet is Christ revealing Himself as King and Priest. To make clear what happens when He reveals Himself, I have to know what He is and does. I distinguish between reality and truth. The truth is the truth of this reality. To speak of truth I have to begin with this reality. Christ's priestly and kingly offices are the subject-matter, the content of His prophetic office, because He reveals Himself. Hence I use this order. In the order of Calvin and other theologians it is never clear what the prophetic office means. Is it the teachings of Christ? What is its connexion with the priestly and kingly offices? I had to change. I begin with the priestly, not the kingly office. This is not an important difference, and I could begin with Christ's kingly action: the elevation of man. Both actions, kingly and priestly, are of equal importance. There are two reasons why I chose the order I use: first, I thought it wiser to begin with God's act for man and then continue with the humanity of Christ and what became of humanity in the sanctified Christ; second, by beginning with the priestly work you can make clear the meaning and reason for the second element, because God did this for man.

S: From a comparison of the architecture, it appears to me that Schleiermacher has carried through his starting-point, the subjective appropriation of revelation, as consistently and beautifully as you have carried through your starting-point, the objective event of revelation. Could it be that your dogmatics is not really in conflict, but is complementary, viewing the same thing from two different angles?

B (shrugging): I could not deny this absolutely. This will be a point to discuss with him later on (in heaven!). But there are differences! I agree that he has done a fine work. I come back again and again to him. He is a brother, but very strange; yet I understand him and why he did it as he did. There is certainly a resemblance in the architecture and system. It is a pity that he is not here to say what he means as he understands it himself. Perhaps the subjective appropriation of revelation has a greater place in my presentation than the objective event of revelation has in his system. I do not find corresponding paragraphs in Schleiermacher to mine on the work of the Holy Spirit in the Church and the individual. If you were right, then Schleiermacher should have given more recognition to the problem of the objective event of revelation.

PART II

Concerning Karl Barth's Church Dogmatics, *Volume I* *'The Doctrine of the Word of God'*

Session 1: Pars. 1 and 2

S: What is the relation of the Church to the world, with its science and philosophy? Why is dogmatics necessary for fruitful contact and conversation?

B: You speak of conversation, but what does this mean? Conversation takes place when one party has something *new* and *interesting* to say to the other. Only then is conversation an event. One must say something engaging and original, something with an element of mystery. The Church must sound strange to the world if it is not to be dull. The Church's language has its own presuppositions. The Gospel is good *news*, news that is not known. Even we Christians will find ourselves in conflict with the Gospel, for it is always news and new for us too. The secularised Church is peaceful, but not a light in the world. The Church must be salt and light, but in order to be these, it must clarify its presuppositions. Thus the necessity of dogmatics! Even philosophers will not listen to a theologian who makes concessions, who is half-philosopher himself. But when you ring the bell of the Gospel, philosophers will listen! For the past two centuries most theologians have been cowards, and the result was that the philosophers despised them. There is no reason for theologians to be afraid. We may read philosophers (and we should!) without accepting their presuppositions. We may listen respectfully (I have a holy respect for a *good* philosopher!). We can learn much from philosophy and science. But as theologians we must be obedient to the Word.

S: On page 28 you quote Karl Heim as saying, 'There falls to Christian philosophy a merely negative task. It must "unsecure" man. It must frankly show up in its impossibility everything that man has at any time undertaken, in order to move into a position in reserve where he is secure in face of the question of eternity, which every moment confronts him with afresh.' Could this not be the answer to the question of the relation of theology to philosophy and science?

19

B: Heim has said that theology can show philosophy and science their limits. Theologians must go with the secularists to the very end and then show them their error. Thus the theologian must only open the question. This is a negative, not a positive, approach! I do not like this procedure! I think it is unfruitful. We must remember that the limits and frontiers of science and philosophy are always moving. Furthermore, is the presupposition true, that at the end of our thoughts we will always meet God? I do not think so. After all, it may be the devil!

S: Can the theologian take philosophy seriously?

B: It is really not my business to accept philosophy. Perhaps it could be accepted as a system of logic, but not as a metaphysic. I myself think the function of philosophy should be to present a sincere *history of philosophy*, that is, to give a review of what man has thought. Philosophy should produce a broad picture of the different thinking of man down through the ages, but always with the presupposition that philosophy can never answer the ultimate question.

S: How would you answer the criticism that your theology is a new mysticism? You say that it is the *Holy Spirit* who makes the Bible God's Word for me, but can we *trust* the Holy Spirit to continue to do this?

B: What an idea of the Holy Spirit, if He cannot be trusted! But the Holy Spirit is *God*, and God *can be* trusted. There is true continuity, but a continuity of the *actions of God*.

Session 2: Par. 3, Sec. 1, pp. 51-67

S: What is the Church's role in regard to social evils?

B: If there is such a thing as proclamation of the Word of God, and if preaching is foremost in proclamation, then it must speak to social situations, since sin is mixed up in the social order. The Gospel enters into the life of man. But social action *must* not be separated from proclamation of the Word; it must be a part of the proclamation. The social work must remain the *Church's* work and not get mixed up and identified with particular parties, world views, and so forth. Certainly, the Christian man must take action, but we are now concerned in this section with the Church's *proclamation*. All I would want to say here is that enjoying Christian freedom and being obedient to God's command are the *same* thing.

S: What should be the attitude of the Church toward art, literature, drama, and so forth? Could these be considered proclamation, or are they propaganda?

B: We must not doubt that the Holy Spirit can work in strange ways. Nevertheless, is the task of the theatre the task of the Church? Where is the commission for the Church to play theatre? I think the existence of *good* Christian authors, painters, actors, and musicians is fine. Indeed, I would prefer these Christians to be very competent and thus by their work to be good witnesses for Christ—not in Christian unions, but individually. However, this does not fulfil the task of the Church.

S: What is the New Testament meaning of *didachē*? What is the connexion between *didachē* and *kerygma*?

B: *Didachē* means 'instruction', understood as an education to reasonable reflection and to gain advice for what man has to do. It is concerned with some existing *authority*. In the time of Jesus the teacher could expound the Old Testament law and prophets. In the New Testament the teacher calls to *repentance*. He asks for reflection and tells what to do. Teaching as such is not a sermon, but expounding the Bible can hardly leave out the call to repentance! Thus the *kerygma* is not without *didachē*. The instruction of youth in the Church is very necessary, especially in our day. They must be taught the books of the Bible and the concerns of Christian doctrine. It is a pity that there are churches that do not know where they stand in regard to doctrine. Yet children want to learn *something*! The over-emphasis of children's instruction is certainly not a danger in our time. We need to take a sober view of education. The Roman Catholics know how to instruct children, and they are advancing everywhere. Their propaganda will increase in the days ahead. We Protestants must use our *brains*, not just 'faith' and 'love'!

S: Do you think communion should be administered every Sunday?

B: Yes, I do. It should be the climax of every service. Calvin asked the government of Geneva to have communion every Sunday, but the government refused. This began the tradition of infrequent communion in the Reformed Church.

S: But if communion were introduced into the service every Sunday, would not the sermon have to be reduced to, say, 20 minutes?

B: This would be too much like the Roman Catholics! We must not reduce the length of the sermon. Services would have to be $1\frac{1}{2}$ to 2 hours long. Sermons should be no less than 30 minutes long—between 30 and 45 minutes, I would say.

S: Is there preaching in the Church that does not reach fulfilment in the sacramental sphere?

B: When we preach we do the same thing as the Roman Catholic priest when he is celebrating the transubstantiation. We should not give people less than the Roman Catholic Church gives. We must help men and women to meet God. We have not less duty than the Roman Catholics, but *more*. In the Roman Church liturgy makes sense because it has a centre. Where is Protestantism's concrete centre?

S: What do you think of the practice of some Anglicans who celebrate the Lord's Supper every day with only the words of institution?

B: I do not like it. It is too private. The Lord's Supper means we are together as the family of the Father. There is no such thing as self-communion. Such an idea is something mystical, mysterious, heathen—perhaps entering into Christianity in the second century.

Session 3: Par. 3, Sec. 1, pp. 67-79

S: What is the point in sacramental theology? My question is directed towards the practice in the Iona Community. Is the whole universe redeemed, so that all material things can be sacramental? And what about *offering*, in the sense that man brings something to the Church, where God blesses it and gives it a special meaning?

B: This practice is very interesting, for it is a great play between God and man. It may be very edifying. But where is the New Testament command from Jesus Christ? What shall be the centre of the life of the Church? This type of sacramentalism (offering) puts man in the centre of the service. This offering would be a new sacrifice, but the *one* sacrifice has been made. The primary function of the Church is proclamation, not answering. I do not want to explain even the Lord's Supper in a sacramental way. The Lord's Supper was just a meal of fellowship, and wine and bread were simply the common food. We must not give special importance to bread and wine.

Emphasis on bread and wine is not New Testament, but cosmic philosophy.

S: On page 70 you quote Paul Tillich as saying, '*Verbum* is more than *oratio.*' Is he not right in saying that the Word is present not only where it is spoken and conceived, but also where it is made visible in symbols? Are there not legitimate symbols in the Bible itself, such as the cross and the dove? Why does Protestantism not employ visible symbols?

B: I do not like the idea of symbols! We do not believe in symbols. We are trying to repeat what we have heard, to testify to what God has done, to proclaim what we are told to proclaim. Symbols are a philosophical means of communicating. Are we told to have or to employ symbols, such as a crucifix or candles? Is there any serious reason for making use of these in the service of the Word? Is there a divine command; is there an example in the Bible? We are *told* to testify by our lives, to live within the community of the Church, to take part in the work of proclamation. But who is told to light candles? If St. Paul came back, he would find our Church service dull, but he would not suggest that we light candles! Read 1 Corinthians 12 and Romans 12. What we need is the Holy Spirit and His gifts! To change to pictures, symbols, and so forth, would be like a sick man in the hospital who wants to change his bed.

S: Should the reformation of the Roman Catholic Church be carried out by the abolition of liturgy or a reformation of the Mass with the correct insertion of preaching? Would not the second way be a chance for ecumenical contact between Protestantism and Catholicism?

B: You cannot reconsider the Mass without reconsidering the *centre* of the Mass and its whole theology (the offering).

Session 4: Par. 3, Sec. 2

S: This question concerns 'systematic theology'. What is the difference between a theology that is systematic and a theology that is a system?

B: We must distinguish at least three uses of the term 'systematic': (1) systematic as regards orderly and thoughtful organisation of material; (2) systematic in that it claims to be exhaustive in its interest, believing that revelation has something to say to all areas of life; (3) systematic in the sense of being derived from a main principle or group of principles. I will admit that the *Church Dogmatics* is systematic in the first two senses, but not in the last. You may know, however, that I have been heavily attacked by the Dutch Calvinists, who say that, in the last analysis, I am a philosopher—indeed an 'existentialist'! —and that my Christological centre is really an ontological, noetic principle. This is certainly the last thing that I intend: to turn theology into a 'system'. In the end, the Bible affords the only criterion for judging whether or not my theology is a system. I try to think orderly, but in a *human* orderliness. I start with the Word, with Christ. I write in terms of the Bible. And yet I know that no theological work can be infallible. My theology is not written in heaven, but in Basel; not by an angel, but by a man. When I depart from the Holy Spirit, then I can be called a philosopher. The Holy Spirit does not like a 'system'—not even a Christological one!

S: In the 1920's your theology was called 'dialectical'. Since I have never been able to understand why it was so designated, I am wondering about the origin of the term.

B: I myself was the originator of this unfortunate term, as you will discover if you read *The Word of God and the Word of Man*. In a lecture to some fellow ministers on 'The Word of God and the Task of the Ministry', I opposed the dogmatic and mystical ways of understanding the relation between God and man and advocated the dialectical way. It was not to be positivistic, not self-critical, not mystical—but dialectical! I have long ago lost interest in the word, however.

S: Does God voluntarily submit His Word to man's limitations?

B: Yes, but the Word still remains *free*. We are not the master, but the servant of the Word.

S: In speaking on page 80 of the Church's responsibility for proclamation, you cite several ways of putting this question that ought to be dismissed, such as when the proclamation is judged according to its agreement with the demands of this or that scientific or aesthetic culture or according to its contribution towards the preservation of this or that form of society or economy, and so forth. 'Far better none at all, than proclamation like that,' you say. What do you really mean?

B: I mean that the Church cannot have two Lords. In America, for instance, is the Church free to preach the Lord, or

24

must it also preach the 'American way of life'? There can be only *one standard* for the Church. Better silence than to preach strange gods! A 'Baal' Church is a greater offence to God than no Church at all. The Church that has no prophetic function is no Church.

Session 5: Par. 4, Sec. 1

S: In paragraph 4 you speak of the Word of God in its threefold form, and you approach the subject in this order: preached Word, written Word, revealed Word. Why do you use this order here, when in Volume I, Part 2, and elsewhere in the *Church Dogmatics*, you use the reverse order, namely, Christ, Scripture, Proclamation?

B: This is because in this first section we are in an introduction, and we must start where we are. Thus I begin with analysis and end with synthesis. In this way I can begin with the proclamation of the Word and end with the same, without repeating myself. The first chapter is merely an *approach* to the subject.

S: How can these sentences on page 102 be understood: 'It (the Word of God) must become the object of human perception if it is to be capable of being proclaimed. But so far as it is really proclaimed, it completely ceases to be the object of human perception'? My disagreement is with the second sentence, which sounds like a docetic idea of revelation.

B: In the first sentence the idea is not capability, but one of intention. The Word of God can only be *believed*, not perceived. It is an object that is different from all other objects; we have it because it gives itself. The point is not the human action, but the Word of God in the human action. This accords with my understanding of the relationship between the divine and human natures in Christ; I give priority to the divine over the human. Forgiveness is felt and known and *believed*, but never within the realm of perception. This does not imply mysticism, however, for it is never separated from the preaching.

S: You say that the Church is an 'event' that happens from time to time, namely, when the proclamation 'happens' or becomes 'event'. If this is so, then where and what is the Church 'when the Church is not the Church', that is, between these happenings?

B: The Church is constantly going forward to this happening

25

of proclamation. The Church is always becoming the Church. It is always being reformed. It lives in *remembering* and *expecting*, between past and future proclamation.

S: On what grounds did the Reformers still regard the Roman Church as a *Church*, though apostate?

B: Not because it was an ecclesiastical institution, but because in it there is reading of Scripture and the administration of Baptism and the Lord's Supper.

S: Ought we not to enter the pulpit with the *expectation* that God will speak through us? Ought we not to hope?

B: You ought to underscore the word 'hope'. When Luther, near the end of his life, scribbled, 'We are really beggars,' he was not in despair. Being a beggar before God means being a child of God!

S: What is the relation of the ongoing presence of the Spirit in the Church and the coming of Christ in preaching and sacrament?

B: The Holy Spirit is a gift to the Church which must be revived on particular occasions. God does not make a nuisance of Himself in order to be continually adored. He is present as Spirit when Christ is proclaimed, but not as some ethereal substance.

Session 6: Par. 4, Sec. 2

S: Do you not think that Protestants put too much emphasis upon the Bible?

B: Protestants need not be ashamed of the Bible (I think of those who say 'life' and not a 'book', 'reality' and not 'words'!). Without the Bible over against the Church, then we are in the Roman Catholic camp. The Bible must always be over against the interpreting Church. This is the reason for exegesis. The Bible must be free, that is, sovereign, over against the Church.

S: What gives the present canon of Holy Scripture its authority?

B: There is no explanation for authority. The canon is the canon just because it is so.

S: What differentiates your understanding of the Word of God from that of a fundamentalist?

B: For me the Word of God is a *happening*, not a thing. Therefore the Bible must *become* the Word of God, and it does this through the work of the Spirit.

S: Why do we Protestants not include the Apocrypha or other writings within the canon?

B: The books of the Bible have forced themselves upon the Church, and in the canon the Church has recognised that this is true. The Church has heard the witness of the Holy Spirit. But has the Church heard the Holy Spirit aright? We cannot be too sure. There is the possibility of human error. The question must remain open. The Church simply confesses its belief in the authority of the twenty-seven books of the New Testament. But if some authentic manuscript from the hand of one of the disciples—say, a Gospel written by Peter—were discovered, then the Church, through the action of some appropriate ecumenical council, could certainly add this to our present canon. Barring some such discovery, I do not think the canon will be changed for two reasons: first, a bad one: because the relation of the Church to the Holy Spirit is not too good; and second, a good one: because the Old Church may have been right!

S: What is the value of textual criticism?

B: The variants are very old commentaries on the text.

Session 7: Par. 4, Secs. 3 and 4

S: Why does the Holy Spirit not appear more explicitly in this section on the 'revealed Word'?

B: You must remember the theological situation in 1932. At that time I wanted to place a strong emphasis on the objective side of revelation: Jesus Christ. If I had made much of the Holy Spirit, I am afraid it would have led back to subjectivism, which is what I wanted to overcome. Today I would speak more of the Holy Spirit. Perhaps I was too cautious. You students should not make that mistake in your polemical writings!

S: Do you think it is time for theology to be based on the Doctrine of the Holy Spirit?

B: A good theology can be based on any of the three articles of the Creed. You could base it on the Doctrine of the Holy Spirit. I now think that a good Doctrine of the Holy Spirit would have been the best criticism of Schleiermacher and of all Modernism, better than my own attack on Schleiermacher. A good critique of Bultmann and existential theology would lie along this same line. Schleiermacher must be understood as one who made a great attempt to centre theology on the Holy

27

Spirit, but in the wrong way. Thus it was a great failure; but we should appreciate the attempt! I personally think that a theology of the Spirit might be all right after A.D. 2000, but now we are still too close to the eighteenth and nineteenth centuries. It is still too difficult to distinguish between God's Spirit and man's spirit!

S: Can a theology of the Holy Spirit be based on the objective instead of the subjective side, that is, from God's side apart from man?

B: I do not see how it could be. The Holy Spirit within the Trinity marks the point where the Trinity meets man. How could you have a Doctrine of the Holy Spirit except in connexion with man?

S: On page 136 you state that the Doctrine of the Word of God in its threefold form (revelation, Scripture, proclamation) is the sole analogy to the Doctrine of the Trinity (Father, Son, Holy Spirit). Wherein lies the similarity and wherein the dissimilarity?

B: In the Doctrine of the Trinity all three 'persons' are the same God, and in the Doctrine of the Word of God all three forms are the same Word. But the Son and the Holy Spirit do not 'become' God, whereas Scripture and proclamation must 'become' Word of God. The Son and the Spirit are God, and yet they are distinct from the Father and from each other. The Father 'engenders' the Son, but not the Spirit. The Spirit is 'sent'. The distinction is necessary, although no one—not even Augustine—knows exactly why, that is, can explain the difference.

S: What objection do you have to so-called 'existential exegesis'?

B: The existential exegete presupposes not only his own dialogue with the text, but a specific anthropology, that is, a pattern of thought. In my case mistakes are possible; in the existentialist's case mistakes are necessary.

Session 8: Par. 5, Secs. 1 and 2

S: Is not the need for revelation, as distinct from revelation itself, given in experience? That is, is not Augustine right when he says, 'Our hearts are restless until they find their rest in Thee'? And is there not a place for correlation, as in Tillich?

B: If we experience a need, do we not know something regarding *what* we need? I cannot accept a division between revelation and the *need* of it. The need is only experienced by those who know revelation. God's answer awakens the question. You cannot seek God before you have found Him, and you cannot find Him before you are found by Him. *Then* you see the real question. There are many false questions, you know. In regard to the quotation from Augustine, remember that his *Confessions* were written during his Platonic period. What or who is 'Thee'? Is it Pascal's God: the God of Abraham, Isaac, and Jacob? Or is it the Platonic reminiscence: we remember our profound unity with God and we have no rest until we return to the beginning of our existence? In his *Confessions* there is always the question whether Augustine is not really writing as a philosopher. Concerning your last question, I see no good way to find a correlation between philosophical questions and theological answers. If God is what Plato or my friend Paul Tillich calls God, then there is a correlation. But if God is He who speaks through prophets and apostles, then the solution is not so simple and easy to find. As I have said before, I have a holy respect for a good philosopher—and I admire my friend Paul Tillich. But I do not think he is writing Christian theology. In this natural realm there is no such thing as a 'creature' or a 'Creator'. If I understand myself as a creature, then I understand my limits and He who limits me: God the Creator. We are either in this circle of knowledge or we are not. That is the question of revelation or faith.

S: This question concerns the form and content of the Word of God. If we can only know the content of the Word of God indirectly, that is, as a 'reflected image' inferred from its forms (pp. 149-50), then what is the formal basis of this indirect knowledge? Is it based on analogy? I know that you oppose *analogia entis* (analogy of being), but assume that you support *analogia fidei* (analogy of faith). Can you explain more fully what this means?

B: Even for indirect knowledge there must be something common to the Word and to us. There must be an analogy between the reflected image and the thing itself. But the word 'analogy' is burdened with Roman Catholic connotations, since they affirm an *analogia entis*. The whole natural theology of the Roman Catholic Church is based on the supposition that there is an analogy of being (*esse*). God *is* and the creature *is*—in a different manner, certainly, but both *are*. So there is something in common between them. If I have the right idea of *esse*, I know something regarding God and the creature, and I can attempt to deepen the idea of being and then attain a certain knowledge of created things and the Creator. So in Roman Catholicism man has a grip on God in this idea of being. I oppose *analogia entis* because 'being' is a purely philosophical notion not at all concerned with the character of God and the creature. It is only an abstract thing that cannot be made fundamental to the knowledge of them both. I do support *analogia fidei*, an analogy of faith. When I point to three forms of the Word of God, I point to three places where the event of the knowledge of relationship between God and man will happen. In this event there will be an analogy between God and man, but it is an analogy that is established by God Himself. In these three forms the opportunity for a real relationship is present, because it is here that the act of God's speaking and man's hearing will take place.

S: In the Bible human words are used. We suppose we speak the truth when we are true to the Bible. But on what grounds?

B: We may suppose there is truth in our human words when they are spoken in the faith that is given by God Himself. In the context of this event, there is truth.

S: In this section on the nature of the Word of God, why did you not simply begin with the statement: 'The Word of God is Jesus Christ,' and let the rest of the section be an elaboration of that?

B: That would be an improvement. The Christological character of the *Church Dogmatics* is perhaps not so clear in Volume I as it should be! But, pedagogically, there is a certain advantage in beginning with hesitation and then ending with equation.

S: I can understand how Church proclamation and Holy Scripture are *language* in the literal sense of the word, but I cannot understand how *revelation* can be considered as language in the same *literal* sense. Is this not too limiting, in view of the fulness and richness of the revelation in Jesus Christ: His life, death, resurrection, and particularly His present life in the Church? For instance, would we not say that the Word of God in the sacraments is more than language?

B: Look at the first sentence of section 3: 'Where God speaks, it is meaningless to cast about for the corresponding act.' It happens in the sphere of language—yes, in the literal sense—but it is the language of God. The language of God is nowhere without human language. You cannot divide the Word of God from human words. Think of the Prophets: 'Thus says the Lord:'—and then followed their Hebrew words! I do not think there is a Word of God alone—a Godly Word. Our praying is an attempt to speak to God. Our hearing is only an attempt. Our preaching is an attempt. But the attempt must be made. By means of this attempt God speaks!

S: Are there not things that cannot be put into words?

B: Certainly. Words only point, but it must be done. The Cross is a Word of God and therefore a Word for us, but not apart from the witness of Holy Scripture and proclamation. The Word in the sacraments (I do not like this term 'sacrament'!) is not more than language, but another form of language. And the sacraments are not without words.

S: But the literal word appeals to the *rational* part of man.

B: Oh! And you object to that? We are either wholly rational or not rational at all! All that happens to man has to come through his *ratio*.

S: On page 152 we find the statement that the Word of God is 'primarily spiritual'; then on the following page it is said to be a 'rational and not an irrational event'. Do 'spiritual' and 'rational' mean the same thing to you? If not, what is the difference? I am concerned because some people charge you with promoting irrationalism in theology, whereas others believe your theology is basically rationalistic!

B: In this context 'spiritual' (*geistige*, not *geistliche*) and 'rational' mean the same thing. Concerning *reason*, I want to say this: I will have nothing to do with the distrust of reason. I have great trust in reason. I am not a rationalist, but I believe that the reason is a good gift of God and that we must make full use of it in theology. This is our praise of God, who has given us this gift to distinguish that two and two equals four instead of five. That is my rationalism! Some people want to make reason the abstract judge of all—and that is unreasonable!

S: On page 151 we find a primary emphasis on the spirituality of the Word of God, as distinguished from any physical event. You hasten to add, however, that there is no Word of God without a physical event. Would this imply that the Word of God was any *less* the Word *before* the Incarnation? Would it imply that the existence of 'addressees' of the Word is, after all, in some way constitutive for the concept of the Word of God, an idea that you reject later in the chapter (page 158)?

B: I do not see why. Before the Incarnation the Word of God was concerned with Incarnation. Think of the Word spoken in the history of Israel: the outspoken physical event at the Red Sea! The Exodus later became the centre of the whole memory of the people of Israel; not the event as such, but the event as the *materia* of this Word of God. It is a good thing that we have the Old Testament with so many tangible things, so that we see that the Gospel is not purely a spiritual thing, merely for soul and heaven. Rather, it is for soul and *body*, heaven and *earth*, inward and *outer* life. There is no hair on my head that is not an interesting thing for God! Also, think of the New Testament miracles. The Saviour is concerned with illness and physical death. Here we have much to learn from the Eastern Orthodox Church. We tend to think in religious, moral, social, psychological terms, not in terms of the *whole* man. We must be concerned with the whole man: as a rational being on this earth, with two feet planted here. Redemption is redemption of the whole man: bodily resurrection. The Word of God as such cannot be understood exclusively from the spiritual side; primarily, yes, but not exclusively.

Session 9: Par. 5, Sec. 3

S: What is the relation between God's language and God's mighty acts? Is not the primary character of revelation *action* rather than language? For example, think of the passion of Jesus.

B: God's language and action are one and the same thing. God's act is God's Word; God's Word is God's action. We speak of the same reality and therefore not of a relationship, since they are not different. In Luke, Jesus is described as one 'mighty in word and deed'. For the Gospels all the actions of Jesus are one reality, seen from different points of view or aspects. There is not one word of Jesus that is not also an action. In His resurrection the whole of His life becomes Word through the power of the Holy Spirit. The Exodus is the con-

32

stituting act of the Old Testament, and the history of Israel may be understood as the exegesis of this act. But this act must be understood. It is the prophets who make it understood. We do not have Exodus *and* prophecy in the Old Testament. Both are together. The Exodus is the prophecy of God. God's action is not primary over God's speech. Here there is no primary or secondary. In my *Prolegomena* I have had to centre my attention on God's *Word*, but this does not mean that 'Word' is a primary category. In Volume II God Himself is primary, in Volume III the work of the Creator, etc. But more and more Jesus Christ is seen as the centre. In dogmatics there is a changing movement in which the same reality is taken into account from different aspects. There is no hierarchy in Christian topics. There is only one truth, one reality, but different views, different aspects: just like the sun shines on different places.

S: You say that in the *Prolegomena* to the *Church Dogmatics* the 'Word' is made central on purpose. Is the reason perhaps because the Word is central in the Church?

B: The Word is central only when the task of dogmatics is concerned, not necessarily in the Church altogether. Of course there is an emphasis on the Word in Protestantism, but there is no metaphysical principle of 'Word'.

S: But would you say that God could act through our acts, instead of His speaking through our words?

B: I would not exclude this, but here in this section I must be concerned with the role of dogmatics in the Church. I would have to explain what 'action' means if I accepted your statement, and then I would have to say that the action is the preaching of the Word! I am not a Catholic.

S: What about healing? This is an action.

B: Let us suppose that there is such a thing as a healing ministry. If this healing ministry is in a legitimate connexion with the healing ministry of Christ, then this healing can only be put into action in the sense of being a witness in the world. A minister cannot improve the world, but he can be an important witness to the power of Jesus. And if you explain healing, you have to exegete, and then you are back to the Word!

S: Can we not repeat the actions of God in ethics?

B: I do not like this word 'repetition'. This is a term that is too coloured by its use in Roman Catholicism; they also think of an ethic of following in footsteps, repeating acts of Christ. But this is not the meaning of Paul. As disciples we are called to witness; we cannot do the same acts as Christ.

S: The task of the Church is proclamation, but does this take place only in the sermon?

B: No, but in dogmatics we are connected with the sermon. In the life of the Church, dogmatics is related to the teaching of the Church, where the Church needs thoughts and words: not just acts, but also activity of the brain. This is the *doctrinal* side of the life of the Church. Perhaps you have understood me more dogmatically than I am. I appreciate the other aspects of the Church's life.

S: On page 164 you speak of three times: the time of Jesus Christ, the time of apostolic testimony, and the time of the Church. Are there Christological parallels to these 'times', e.g. resurrection: the time of the apostles; ascension: between the times, Christ removed from the world; second coming: Christ heard and understood by all men?

B: Yes, why not? Such parallels are possible. Perhaps there are others. What about the work of Christ as priest, king, and prophet? Or the analogy of the Trinity? Why not? But we must be clear about the fact that this is a kind of intellectual play. But if these parallels are illuminating, then they *may* be not only examples, but also a confirmation of the inner necessity of the choice of these three times. But it can only be a *confirmation*. You cannot *begin* with these parallels, but you may find them afterwards.

S: In emphasising that God's Word is an act or event, you say that it has a *contingent* character, that it is 'contingently contemporaneous'. The contingent character is seen from our side, but is it not removed or modified from God's side by His faithfulness? And does not 'contingent' mean 'without reason'?

B: But there is a reason behind this event! When I use 'contingent', I wish to say that God's act cannot be put in the framework of the 'general'. But why would this event-character exclude God's faithfulness? By no means! This event as such is the revelation of God's faithfulness! When God acts or speaks, He does so as the faithful God. This is the meaning of God's action and Word. No one can doubt it; He will fulfil His promise. But the Word of God is always *aimed*! It is not like fireworks, but like a gun that is aimed and shot at a definite time and in a definite situation. No generalities, like 'love', 'peace', 'essence', 'highest being'. The Word of God is not *generally* understandable.

S: What effect can God's Word have in ruling those outside the Church, that is, the whole world?

B: If you do not make a distinction between God's Word and God's power, then you can believe that God's Word rules the whole world, the world under the Lordship of Christ. Think of St. Paul. He believed in this power, and he had to explain it to his world. The reality of Jesus' Lordship comes before the world knows it. It is not to be explained as possibility; it is reality.

S: But does it rule the world as revelation?

B: Yes, but revelation is power. Think of light coming into darkness, and darkness cannot overthrow it. His shining overcomes the darkness. Think of the prologue of John: all has been created through the *Logos*, and the *Logos* is Jesus Christ. When we speak of Jesus Christ as the Word, everything is possible.

Session 10: Par. 5, Sec. 4

S: In the incarnation you say that God veils Himself and at the same time unveils Himself. Is the 'veiling' Jesus of Nazareth and the 'unveiling' God's eternal Son? If so, why is it not said more explicitly?

B: So you would have liked me to speak more Christologically! I hesitate to accept your statement, because the manhood of Christ is not to be thought identical with the veiling character of the Word of God. If you consider Christology from the point of view of the condescension of the Word of God, God becoming flesh, then you are right. But there is another way to see the manhood of Christ: as the unveiling of God. Christ in His resurrection is the unveiling of God. There is no 'law' to distinguish between veiling and unveiling. These are not two parts, but only two moments in this event. Look at Peter's confession: 'You are the Christ!' In Christ there is ontological unity, but for Peter this unity is only in faith.

S: If you are studying the words of Paul, will there be any given moment when the words of Paul become identical with the Word of God *for you*?

B: No. For *you* there may be unity, but not identity.

S: On page 198 you speak of God's Word being either veiled or unveiled. Is not the Word fully veiled *and* unveiled, rather than veiled *or* unveiled? This is what I gather from reading about this matter in your Doctrine of God, Volume II, Part 1.

B: Here I must say veiled *or* unveiled, because I want to stress the *moment*, the one-sidedness of the Word. Here I want to distinguish between the moment of veiledness and the moment of unveiledness. But when I speak of veiling and unveiling in the section on the knowledge of God in Volume II, then I am in the context of the notion of God Himself, and there I must stress the *unity*.

S: On page 205 you give biblical examples of the mysterious 'one-sidedness' of the Word of God. For instance, you point out the impossibility of synthesising or harmonising the covenant of Sinai (Exodus 19-20) with the covenant of Jeremiah (Jeremiah 31), and yet both are Word of God. But cannot the unity of the witness in the Old Testament and in the New Testament be proved by exegesis?

B: When I wrote this I was inclined to see the differences in the two covenants. You should also look at what I say about 'covenant' in Volume IV, Part 1. There I tried to see some points of unity, but I do not know whether my colleague Walter Baumgartner would agree! It is an open question. Perhaps here I have spoken too confidently about this hypothesis. Now I am more sceptical. Exegetically a certain unity of the witness can be shown, but the point of union can only be understood by faith. For instance, this would be true in the case of the witness of John that the Son of God is *Jesus of Nazareth*, and the Synoptic witness that Jesus of Nazareth is the *Son of God*. The subject of the New Testament is Jesus Christ, and that can be understood only by faith. Exegetically you can find quite different opinions about Christ. An exegesis cannot be complete without the *kerygma*, and the *kerygma* can only be *believed*. Nevertheless, faith cannot be a substitute for good historical and critical work in exegesis.

S: When you conceived the three forms of the Word of God (Jesus Christ Himself, Holy Scripture, and proclamation) did you mean to include the sacraments in them?

B: Sacrament is included in the preached Word.

S: What do you think about the Quakers' 'inner light'?

B: Quakers are such good people, I do not like to criticise

them, but I do not think their theology is so good. There might be another spirit besides the Holy Spirit speaking in my heart. The Bible is a much more certain source of revelation. Read John, chapter 1, for an understanding of the 'true light'.

S: What do you mean when you speak of the 'openness' of man for the Word of God?

B: The Holy Spirit is the Lord not only of the Word itself, but also of its being heard. Thus I mean openness of mind. The Holy Spirit opens the mind of man to receive and hear the Word.

Session 11: Par. 6, Secs. 1-3

B (introductory remarks): This paragraph on Word and experience has special relevance for the debate regarding the *Church Dogmatics* and the theology behind it. Is this answer regarding experience satisfying in the Anglo-Saxon world? Is not thankfulness enough content for the 'dignity' of man over against God? Even talk of a 'point of contact' is all right, but one given by God!

S: We receive freedom from the free grace of God, who allows us to be men. We are free to say *'yes'* to God. If we say 'no', we make no use of the freedom given to us. My question is this: Saying 'no' may not be freedom, but does it mean going back to prison?

B: The decisive point is whether freedom in the Christian sense is identical with the freedom of Hercules: choice between two ways at a crossroad. This is a heathen notion of freedom. Is it freedom to decide for the devil? The only freedom that means something is the freedom to be myself as I am created by God. God did not create a neutral creature, but *His* creature. He placed him in a garden that he might build it up; his freedom is to do that. When man began to discern good and evil, this knowledge was the beginning of sin. Man should not have asked this question about good and evil, but should have remained in true created freedom. We are confused by the political idea of freedom. What is the light in the Statue of Liberty? Freedom to choose good and evil? What light that would be! Light is light and not darkness. If it shines, *darkness is done away with*, not proposed for choice! Being a slave of Christ means being free.

S: Churches ask questions regarding one's religious experience and call to the ministry. If a genuine experience is not possessed, how does the Church protect itself in regard to a ministry with good moral behaviour and theological education?

B: A confession of faith, religious experience as such, is good. There is no faith without experience. But a candidate for the ministry speaks of *faith*, not of experience as such. He gives an answer to what he has heard of the Word of God.

S: What do you think about preaching for decisions in Revivals?

B: That is a question of pedagogy, tact, psychology, and of the concrete situation. I do not like it as a *system* of evangelisation. I do not pronounce a prohibition to extraordinary men like Moody, who can do what cannot generally be done. All methods are problematic. As a venture, yes. Exclude appeals and you have an ecclesiastical fortress: preaching, prayer, worship. Some want to come out of the fortress and fight. The Apostles did not ask people whether they would accept or not, but told them of reality, not in a sense of false freedom but of true freedom. Concentrate on teaching and preaching the Word of God, and let experience take care of itself. And what I say in the *Church Dogmatics* is not something to preach. These volumes are for your study. When you go into the pulpit, go with the Bible and the Holy Spirit!

S: Does the Word get through in spite of our language?

B: We must use understandable language. You must know your people. The question of the 'point of contact' is not between preacher and hearers, but between the Word of God and man. It is a work of charity for one to address himself to man as pastor, but that charity is not a guarantee of the Word. The pastor is only a minister of the Word. What effect has our preaching on the coming of the Word? It may be that our preaching is bad; nevertheless, it is possible that through our ineffectively preached words and bad language, the Holy Spirit may speak. We must *obey* and do our best to be understood! In logic, point comes before reality. In this passage I say the opposite. I draw my categories of logic from the Bible. Is God far away, beyond a chasm? I do not begin with the chasm, but with Christ who bridges it. But *in Him* I see the infinite apartness of God and man, when I see what is overcome. It is important to see the aloofness of God in order to be thankful. Better than comfortably to say: 'God is not so far!' God has done for us what is impossible, and has made it both possible *and real*! God is with us, but as the God in the highest. Glory to God in the highest, and on earth peace to men—they cannot be separated! That is not a philosophical dialectic, but the content of the whole Bible.

Session 12: Par. 6, Sec. 4

S: In the Fall does not man lose an ontological relation with God, an *analogia entis* grounded in God's grace, rather than an *analogia fidei*?

B: What man has lost in the Fall is his *faith*, not some ontological relation. He has lost his relation as an obedient child of God and has gone out of *analogia fidei*.

S: This question concerns the fulfilment of faith. What room is left for fulfilment of faith in the *eschaton*, if faith is really God Himself?

B: Faith is only one of the words used in the New Testament in speaking of the relation of God and man. There is also hope and love. Faith is a limited and not an unlimited notion. Nevertheless, faith can be used to describe the *whole*, but viewed from a *spatial* aspect. The biblical meaning gives room for fulfilment. Faith is not vision, is not completion. Faith cannot be without hope and love. Being perfect in itself, it is yet lacking because it does not view the whole, and this is also true of the notions of hope and love. Christian truth has many aspects. But there will be no need for dogmatics in heaven!

S: Is not faith, even 'perfect faith', tainted by *sin* in this life?

B: I can talk about *faith* as perfect, but there is no *man* who has perfect faith. Faith is a perfect gift of God, but *my* faith is only a small reflection of this gift.

S: Concerning *nurture*: If God Himself comes in the knowledge of God and if faith is perfect, wherein comes the chance for growth and maturity?

B: Knowledge and faith come *to us*, and we have to study and live under the Word of God. Now not only the possibility, but the necessity of growth is declared.

S: Why have Christian education?

B: Seen from God's side, God is free and all else means nothing. But God gives us opportunity in the world to be witnesses. God invites us to be *active* with Him (even when we write long dogmatics!). All this work we do can only be done as a service, not as a pragmatic device, as if we could build up the Kingdom. We can only *proclaim* the Kingdom. When God works through a man, it is always a *miracle*. We can only be *obedient* ministers of the Word of God. We can make no *claims*.

S: This question concerns the unity of the Church. What is the relation between the perpendicular and the horizontal: the self-revelation of God from above and the historical ongoing of the Church?

B: Jesus Christ is the same yesterday, today, and for ever. He Himself is the historical continuity of the Church. He is present in the Holy Spirit. Suppose there is a history of the outpouring of the Spirit within the historical series of the events of the Church. Then you have an unbroken continuity of the presence of the Word of God. The visible Church, the human efforts, is to be believed, but you must see more than this. You must see the work of the Spirit.

S: This question concerns the justice of God. Because some men are not Christians and their being Christians depends on God's own revelation, then is God unjust? What does this say about missions?

B: The motive for missions is the concern for telling others that God has shown His grace to *all*. Take the example of St. Paul. He *had* to witness, for he saw a world of people who had not heard the 'good news'. The Church knows that God does not fail to show His grace. The Church must proclaim. The answer cannot be a theoretical but a practical one. A true missionary can never believe that those who refuse the Gospel can really refuse. He does not know on what ground the seed falls. Only then can a missionary be really free. He is only an ambassador, not the king.

Session 13: Review Pars. 1-6

S: When this volume was written in 1932, you said that the chief heresies you had in mind when writing were Roman Catholicism and Modernism. Would you still use these today, or have other opponents arisen?

B: If I had to rewrite this volume, I might not be so polemical, although the heresies would be the same. I might have a more irenic spirit. I could look out on the present situation and ask: what should the Christian proclamation be in view of all these denominations in the Ecumenical Movement, etc.? But maybe the way I said it is clearer. Liberalism is coming back today, especially in Europe. Look at Rudolf Bultmann; he stems from Father Schleiermacher! And look at the situation in Switzerland (Martin Werner, Fritz Buri, etc.)! And the old snake in Rome is still there! I might have mentioned a third heresy: Fundamentalism, Orthodoxy. In 1932 I did not know the Fundamentalists so well. The Fundamentalist says he knows the Bible, but he must have become master over the Bible, which means master over revelation. Fundamentalism arose in the last of the seventeenth century at the same time as natural theology, and I consider it just another kind of natural theology: a view of the modern man who wants to control revelation.

S: On page 198 and following you speak of God's language as God's mystery in its one-sidedness, and you relate 'veiling' and 'unveiling', 'form' and 'content', and so forth. Can the relation of justification and sanctification also be subsumed under 'mystery' in the same way?

B: Possibly 'veiling' and 'unveiling' would apply, but not 'form' and 'content'. I do not like these latter terms. Justification and sanctification are two aspects of one reality, and we can only see one side at a time. Calvin speaks of one and then the other. I do not believe they can be spoken of in a twofold way. In theology the terms 'form' and 'content' have no place, for they are philosophical distinctions. I am sorry I ever used them!

S: In discussing the 'image of God' on page 273, you say the following: 'What is preserved of the image of God even in sinful man is *recta natura*. . . .' What is this '*recta natura*'?

B: This simply means that man remains man, even as a sinner. *Recta natura* is not the image of God. I think that *imago Dei* is the relation of man and woman. Man is created in an I-Thou relationship similar to the I-Thou relation in God Himself. This likeness cannot be lost. After the Fall man still retains his being as man and still is directed toward God and other men, but he is unable to obtain his goal, unable to reach either God or man.

Session 14: Par. 7, Sec. 1

S: On page 299 you make this statement: 'The Word of God is the speech, the act, the mystery of God, and so not a substance immanent in the Church apart from the event of its being spoken and believed, or discoverable and demonstrable in her. Therefore, even the Church is not constantly, continuously the Church of Jesus Christ, but such she is in the event of the Word of God being spoken to her and believed by her.' But can we not *always* turn to the Bible as the Word of God, and can we not say that the Church is the organic, living association of believers?

B: The Church exists only as an *event* of the Word, and therefore we cannot always turn to the Bible and be sure of receiving the Word of God. Word is a *living* reality, not something abstract. It exists in God's action toward us. We must hear and become obedient. As for what you say about the Church: yes, we can speak of the Church as the sum total of believers, but I do not think this is a clear *theological* definition of the Church. That is a sociological definition. For a theological definition we must begin with Christ, who is not only the founder but also the reality of the Church. We are His body. So we look to Him, and not to us poor creatures. And when we look to Him, we must return to the *Word of God*: the living event of speaking and hearing. Believing in the reality of the Church means believing in Jesus Christ. It is Christ who assembles the Church, who builds it up. The apostolic symbols speak of the Church as one, holy, and catholic. All these notions are correct if you realise that the first meaning of these terms has a *Christological* reference.

S: Does 'Body of Christ' have any sociological meaning for you?

B: Yes, if seen Christologically. The Church is *indirectly* identical with Jesus Christ. He is not without His Body. We believe in the *totus Christus*, and that includes His Body on earth. But it is a living body, so we come back to the notion of event.

S: Is the 'body' an event?

B: Yes, bodily existence is an event.

S: Is it not dangerous to say '*totus Christus*'?

B: No. We are only Christ's Body, not the Head. This means that we can never have a 'head' of the Church on earth; this is the Roman Catholic heresy.

S: But should we say that His Body is not yet perfect?

B: I would rather say, 'His Body is not yet *revealed*.' What we see is imperfection, but what we need is '*apokalypsis*'.

42

S: It seems as if you are making a distinction between the Church and the Body of Christ.

B: Yes, I am. You can speak of a renewal of the Church (indeed, *ecclesia semper reformanda*!), but not of a renewal of the Body.

S: In the Roman Catholic Church the Bible and tradition are put on the same level. What happens to dogmatics when it is only carried on in this context? Does not the Church of today simply accept the theology of the Church of yesterday?

B: Certainly there is in the Roman Catholic Church a codification of tradition and a hardening of lines. The real error of Rome lies deeper than this, however. Roman Catholicism is a terrible thing, because it means the imprisonment of God Himself! It claims to be the possessor of the Holy Spirit and revelation and Jesus Christ Himself. Can there be anything more terrible than the identification of God and man! This is worse than any pantheism! It is the more terrible because it is so pious, so beautiful.

S: But no one is secure against this error.

B: You are exactly right! This is why I expose modern Protestantism, with its 'God in your heart'. If I had to choose between modern Protestantism and Roman Catholicism, I would pick the latter. It is at least impressive and interesting!

S: What do you think about the Mariology of the Roman Catholic Church?

B: It is only in the nineteenth century that the Roman Catholic theologians have developed a real Mariology, although it was known in the Middle Ages. In the past forty years the tempo has increased. I would not be surprised if another dogma came forth proclaiming Mary as co-redemptrix. But the question for us is: Why Mary? I think in the figure of Mary they have a great symbol of a human creature who is in connexion with God and is working with God, as the Pope is with Christ or the saints with God. Roman Catholic thinking is about *co-operation* between man and God. Protestants who talk about 'co-operation' are on the way to Rome. Mary answered the angel of God: 'Behold, I am the handmaid of the Lord.' This answer is a classic expression for a co-operating human being. The Romans emphasise God's grace, but through grace Mary becomes co-operatrix and finally co-redemptrix. If I were a Roman Catholic theologian, I would build up a

43

theology on Mariology. I do not know why it has not been done.

Session 15: Par. 7, Secs. 2 and 3

S: Do you not think we have too much dogmatics and not enough following of Christ? At the Evanston assembly of the World Council of Churches someone said, 'The Word was made theology and did not dwell among us!' Do we have a disincarnate Word of God and not a real incarnation?

B: I am wondering about your idea of incarnation. Incarnation is only Jesus Christ, not a sermon or any other proclamation. The sermon is *testimony* to the incarnation, but the incarnation is once-for-all. (We are not Roman Catholics.) In the witness of the Church I think dogmatics and proclamation are in the same sphere. Because the work of the Church, its proclamation, is human, it needs a corrective, and that corrective is dogmatics. Dogmatics testifies to the humbleness of the Church. We must not loosely use the word 'incarnation', which stems from John 1.14 and which refers to Jesus alone. Dogmatics is only a tool, but if it is a tool, why not have a *good* tool? This means we have to study and prepare, and it means that a school must be a school. The mixture of study and practical life as a pastor, as happens with many students in America, is not good.

Session 16: Par. 8, Secs. 1 and 2

S: On page 367 you speak of two questions that would have to be asked of 'other revelations' if they were to be compared with the biblical revelation. Are you here concerned with a justification of the biblical doctrine of revelation, and thus with apologetics?

B: The two revelations, the biblical and some other, are not to be mixed. Is a half page too much to spend on this matter? Dogmatics will always have an apologetic side. In a certain sense all dogmatics is apologetic, namely, in the sense of setting the limits. But God's revelation defends itself. One of my most famous theological masters is Anselm of Canterbury, who tried to show the *context* of doctrines and to prove the necessity of reconciliation and the existence of God. The beauty of the Christian truth is its *unity*. I am a pupil of Anselm. I wonder what he will say to me in heaven. Even my own brother

Heinrich says I have misunderstood him! Be that as it may; I have *learned* something from Anselm! Let the Christian truth speak for itself. If you try to start with an apologetic interest, you are lost.

S: On page 349 you state that 'Holy Scripture and proclamation must always be *becoming* the Word of God in order to be it.' Do they, then, become 'revelation'? If so, why distinguish between revelation and the Word of God?

B: The Son and the Spirit do not become the Father. Therefore I would say that Scripture and proclamation do not become revelation. They *witness* to the revelation. The 'Word of God' is in three forms, but only one form, Jesus Christ Himself, is identical with 'revelation'.

S: What is the difference between '*Historie*' and '*Geschichte*'?

B: '*Historie*' is something that can be proved by general historical science, whereas '*Geschichte*' is something that really takes place in time and space, but may or may not be proved. The creation story has to do with '*Geschichte*', for instance. It has to do with something that happened and therefore something historical, but something that is not open to historiographical investigation. For me the creation stories are sagas, not myths.

Session 17: Par. 8, Sec. 3

S: If revelation is limited by its being given by God, cannot the *Christian* say with the Psalmist in Psalm 19 that the 'heavens declare the glory of God and the firmament showeth His handiwork', and with St. Paul in Romans 1.19-20, that in His creation God has made Himself known to all men so that all are without excuse for their sin?

B: Yes, the man who stands in the revelation can agree with the Psalmist. But read on in Psalm 19: 'There is no speech, nor are there words; their voice is not heard.' In other words, the creation speaks no word. The Christian does not draw *conclusions* from this. He is not able to *repeat* what heaven tells of God. He can confess God's creation, but he cannot make out of this a separate assertion about God. Read the second part of Psalm 19, where man is confronted by the *revelation* itself. The man who can say the second part can also say the first. In Romans 1.18f Paul clearly says that God was present in His world—yes, in His acts and revelation. But man *did not see*

God's revelation. Paul draws *no conclusion* about this affirmation of God's general revelation. *As a Christian* Paul is willing to admit the revelation of God in the whole world, but he derives no knowledge of God from this. That comes only from Jesus Christ. He says these things for two reasons: to glorify God, and to say that man is without excuse. Yes, a Christian will say this, but he will not become a natural theologian!

S: What about the phrase: '... although they knew God they did not honour him as God...'?

B: Objectively they knew Him and denied Him—*in the same instant*! Suppose you were reading a book in a foreign language. You know the words, but you do not know the grammar and syntax. You know, but you cannot read! That is only a poor illustration, but maybe you see what I mean.

S: Is there a 'Fall' of the outer world as well as a Fall of man?

B: I am not sure. I am not ready to say that there is a 'fallen creation'. I would not deny it, but I cannot affirm it.

S: You speak of an *'analogia relationis'* in connexion with Genesis 1.27 (image of God). Could we also speak of a *'vestigium relationis trinitatis'*?

B: In the relation between man and woman there is a kind of *vestigium*. God is not solitary. God is both I and Thou. What we distinguish between I and Thou is not first a quality of man, but of God. But I did not speak of this in relation to the Trinity. However, God always has an 'other'. God is seen acting in history: over against Israel, over against the Church; and in Jesus Christ He is both God and man. I would not deny that in the background I had in mind a relation also between the Father and the Son, which implies the Holy Spirit. In that extreme way it might be applied to the Trinity. Genesis 1 and 2 are both *anticipations* of the whole history of Israel. Or, the Israelites at least have interpreted their history in the light of these creation sagas.

S: On page 396 you state: 'Revelation will not submit to illustration but only to interpretation.' Do the words 'illustration' and 'interpretation' really carry the meaning you assign to them? Was not Paul illustrating in 1 Corinthians 12.12, where he speaks of the 'Body' of Christ?

B: By interpretation I mean to say *the same thing* in other words; by illustration I mean to say the same thing *in other words*. It is difficult to distinguish between these two, but there is a distinction of *intention*. One who illustrates thinks he *knows* what the text means. An interpreter only tries to express the text. The illustrator is master of the text. His attitude is quite different from that of the interpreter. It is *possible* that you do know the text and can be an illustrator, but your illustration then dominates over the text. Your illustration is so interesting that it begins to have an independent life and really takes the place of the biblical text. Then the world becomes important in itself. Then you have a second source of revelation. This is not always true, of course, but there is a great danger! In real interpretation the interpreter has to sacrifice himself to the text. I believe Bultmann is more an illustrator than an interpreter. It is *always a man*, of course, who either illustrates or interprets. The only question is what you will do. The interpreter listens to the text. Is Paul using an illustration when he speaks of 'Body'? Certainly 'body' is an element of our language. But the Body of Christ is not used symbolically. The Body is real.

S: Were the Parables of Jesus illustrations?

B: Jesus mastered the situation. He spoke of the Kingdom of God, and He *was* the Kingdom of God. I am not too sure about the theological character of the Parables.

S: What about when Christ says: 'This is my body; this is my blood'?

B: I think the bread and wine are not to be taken either realistically or symbolically, but that we must see Christ's action as a whole: His action of bringing them all together, of making them His disciples who hear His words and share this table fellowship with Him and receive life from Him. This is what is meant by the breaking of bread and saying, 'This is my body,' and the giving of the wine and saying, 'This is my blood.' The whole controversy over the Lord's Supper is no longer usable for today, because it concerned the wrong thing: the elements. The meaning is to be found in the whole relationship of Christ and the disciples. There is really no difference between the bread and wine. Bread gives nourishment to the body, and wine in Old Testament times was the sign of a festive occasion. Here we think of looking forward to the Messianic Kingdom.

Session 18: Par. 9, Secs. 1 and 2

S: In this section you stress the formula: *Opera trinitatis ad extra sunt indivisa* (the works of the Trinity in an outward direction are undivided). But is there not a distribution economically (*ad extra*)?

B: Yes. Have you read about the doctrine of Appropriations on page 428? And you should see the interpretation of Thomas Aquinas on the following page. The notion of 'Creator' has an analogy to that of 'Father', so that symbolically the Father can be called the Creator. The formula is exact, but within it there are some works that can be attributed to the Father, some to the Son, and some to the Holy Spirit. If this formula were denied, then we would compartmentalise God. There is only one God, but to each 'Person' is attributed certain functions. But they are not *exclusive*.

S: The function of dogmatics is the criticism of proclamation. Would it not be better to build a dogmatics critically (negatively) than to try to make constructive statements?

B: You have forgotten that we are in the *prolegomena* to dogmatics. The Doctrine of the Trinity is used as a critical principle, and you cannot define the principle without entering into theological discussion. This is necessary in order to make clear the principle. The Trinitarian discussion was the first undertaken by the Church, so I believe I also must begin here. My three critical principles are the principle of revelation, the principle of Holy Scripture, and the principle of proclamation, but you cannot define these principles without entering into constructive theology. Of course, naturally I am not an Eastern but a *Western* theologian.

S: Does the *Church Dogmatics* make transcendence epistemological, whereas the Bible makes transcendence ontological, causal, and ethical? You say, for instance, on page 368: 'The revelation attested in the Bible is the revelation of the God who according to His nature cannot be unveiled to man.'

B: The German reads: '*Die in der Bibel bezeugte Offenbarung ist die Offenbarung des seinen Wesen nach den Menschen unenthüllbaren Gottes.*' What I mean is that *man* cannot unveil God. God is incapable of being unveiled *by man*. Otherwise, if God by His own nature could *not* reveal Himself, then we would have no Christianity. God is inaccessible, but this does not mean incapable. It was my task to find out an epistemological concept in the *Prolegomena*. Only then can I go to the whole of God's action. I had to extract a concept of *revelation* from all of God's action as event. One has to work with concepts.

S: But why begin with a *concept*? Why not deal directly with the *event*?

B: The concept I use is a description of the event itself. The result of this investigation of the Doctrine of the Trinity is a *critical principle*.

Session 19: Par. 9, Secs. 3 and 4

S: What is the relation of the doctrines of *Perichoresis* and Appropriations to the human nature of Christ?

B: What do you mean by 'human nature'? Jesus Christ is a 'Person' of the Trinity, but this does not mean that he has a 'personality' in the modern sense of a 'centre of consciousness'. His personality is that of Son of God.

S: But if human nature lacks personality, is it really human nature?

B: Individuality is necessary to human nature, but not Person. A person exists in human nature. Of course Christ had a 'centre of consciousness'. Personality means just this or that man. It can only be applied to the *existence* of a particular man. His thisness or thatness is his personality. If the old Christological doctrine denied personality to Christ, it meant to deny that there was a man as such and then the Word became that man. No, this man never existed except as Son of God—from the beginning. God chose one possibility of humanity out of a mass of possibilities and realised its existence in the Son of God. Humanity means the nature or *essence of man*. Personality means the *existence of a man*. The Father and the Holy Spirit are also concerned in the incarnation (*Perichoresis*), but not so that you can speak of the 'incarnate Father', etc. We might use the illustration of three men: two of them help the other put on a coat, but only this one wears it.

S: Does the incarnation make a change in the Trinity?

B: No, the incarnation makes no change in the Trinity. In the *eternal decree* of God, Christ is God and man. Do not ever think of the second Person of the Trinity as only *Logos*. That is the mistake of Emil Brunner. There is no *Logos asarkos*, but only *ensarkos*. Brunner thinks of a *Logos asarkos*, and I think this is the reason for his natural theology. The *Logos* becomes an abstract principle. Since there is only and always a *Logos ensarkos*, there is no change in the Trinity, as if a fourth member comes in after the incarnation.

S: Was the question of the Doctrine of the Trinity really forced on the Church as an immediate implication of revelation, or was it not rather forced on the Church by the rise of heresy? Your concept of the doctrine as a 'self-enclosed circle' suggests that its function is more negative than positive, namely, to guard the boundaries of Christian proclamation.

B: We cannot make an 'either-or' here. Heresy forced it, but it was an immediate implication of revelation. Also, we must not think of heresy as necessarily bad. Each heresy affords a chance to learn something positive. I have learned much from the 'German Christians' and from Bultmann, for instance. Heresy forces you to search for the truth at its origin and really comes under the category of *God's providence*. Revelation is never exhausted, but must always be understood in a new way. Man is lazy. Heresy pricks him and forces him to open his eyes and ears and to learn. The Reformation would not have been carried through without the deep dissolution of Christian affairs and doctrine in the late Middle Ages. We must not be like Schleiermacher, who made this hard and fast rule: Orthodoxy can never sanction heterodoxy. We cannot make *principles* that measure heresy.

S: What is the difference between your Doctrine of the Trinity and that of Roman Catholicism and Protestant Modernism?

B: In this particular doctrine I am very close to the Roman Catholic doctrine. I think they would probably accept most of my doctrine. An exception would be the third rule added to the Doctrine of Appropriations on page 429. In any case, I am glad to have found such a basic point of agreement with the Roman Church. On this basis we can talk with each other (and I wonder if this is a possibility for Tillich and Niebuhr!). Be glad that the chasm is not so deep here. Modernism has no Doctrine of the Trinity. The notion of a 'Social Trinity' is fantastic!

S: Can you build a Doctrine of the Trinity on the subjective experience of justification instead of on the objective self-revelation of God?

B: Yes, you could start with justification or sanctification. Theoretically, you could move from any point in the dogmatic realm to the Trinity. For me, it was more useful to begin with revelation. However, you could begin your dogmatics with the Doctrine of the Church if you wanted to, and then gradually work back to the ontological Trinity as the source of the existence of the Church.

S: What do you think about Donald Baillie's book, *God Was In Christ*?

B: Donald Baillie is a dear friend of mine, but I have real questions about this book. He tries to explain the two natures of Christ out of the doctrine of grace, and Christology becomes a figure or example or *symbol* of the fact of grace. This is entirely wrong. I would begin with grace, but I would ask, 'The grace of whom?' 'What grace?' I did not like Baillie here.

Session 20: Par. 10, Secs. 1 and 2

B (introductory remarks): Do you like this paragraph on 'God the Father'? I must make a confession. I do not like this paragraph too much, especially the first part! There is nothing false here, but I would not say it this way today. My task was to give an explanation of the Creator, and I said he was 'the Lord of our existence'. This is a remnant of existentialism. My basis is too small. God is Lord not only of *our* existence, but of *all* that is not God. *Our* existence is only a part of what God has created because He did not want to be alone. The *powerful love* of God is the meaning of creation: God's going out from Himself and allowing creation to exist. In order to describe this Lordship of our existence, I have overemphasised eschatology. Here I should not have talked of *eternal life*. I should have talked of *life itself*. I should have said something positive about creation and not just described the qualitative difference between Creator and creature. I could have made the 'affinity' between the relation of the Father to the Son and the relation of the Creator to the creature much clearer if I had spoken of the *love* and *power* of the Father. Here the notion of fatherhood is cold; it does not give the impression of the warm love of the Father. And I should not have spoken here of Golgotha. There is too much notion of death! This reminds me too much of my *Römerbrief*!

S: You said that revelation teaches us that Creator means 'Lord of our existence'. What has this to do with nature?

B: At the time I wrote this I did not know that God was Creator of heaven and earth! Man is too important here. Volume III is a much better presentation of the Doctrine of

Creation. I have learned much! Nature is the theatre of God's work with man. (Remember that man only appears on the afternoon of the sixth day!) The greatness of God's dealing with man is *in nature*. Look in Volume III, Part I, where the first two chapters are devoted to the two creation stories in Genesis. In the first, the creation is the outer ground of the covenant. In the second, the covenant is the inner ground of creation.

S: Does the Father exercise lordship over the Son in the Trinity? And how are we to understand the death of the Son apart from the creature?

B: Yes, there is a fatherly lordship, but I would not like to use this term. Nevertheless, there is a command in the incarnation, and there is a relation of God as Lord and God as Servant. There is no subordination, however. The Christian God can be both: high and low, Lord and Servant. Allah cannot! By the second part of your question, do you imply that God dies in the Son? We must distinguish between God as such and God in His purpose (decree). From eternity the Son (as God *and man*) exists in God. But until the incarnation this has not happened. Nevertheless, this must be made clear; otherwise you have a fourth member in the Trinity. God *does* die in the Son. If this were not so, then we could not say: 'The Son of God has died for us.' Here we remember the lordship of God over life and death. Even the realm of darkness is not outside God's power. God took our place in the realm of death, which is our realm. If we refuse to say that God dies on the cross, then there is no reconciliation.

S: When we look at Golgotha, do we see the eternal relation between the Father and the Son?

B: Yes, in so far as Jesus is a man. Here I should have begun with the *humanity* of Jesus Christ, as in Volume III. Jesus dies two deaths: His own (the first death) and ours (the second death—for *sin*). (Heinrich Vogel does not agree with me here!) These two deaths coincide on the cross. The first is natural death, which belongs to humanity as such. The second is death as God's punishment for the sin of mankind. Jesus dies for *our* sin, though He is sinless.

S: The Father is the 'Originator'. Do we make an appropriation here?

B: No. This is an inner-trinitarian definition. Appropriation applies only *ad extra*.

S: Why do you assign or appropriate 'redemption' to the Holy Spirit rather than to the Son? Is 'redemption' not synonymous with 'reconciliation'?

B: My first reason is exegetical: *apolutrōsis* is an *eschatological* term in the New Testament. Our situation as reconciled men is like that of a man in prison who has received the good news that he is free. The door is open, but he has not yet gone out of prison. Perhaps the word *'Vollendung'* ('consummation') would have been better than *'Erlösung'* ('redemption'). We now *have* freedom, but we are not *in* it! 'Redemption' means more than 'reconciliation', and it has to do with the work of the Spirit. See Romans 8! However, I admit a certain ambiguity in the terms 'redemption' and *'Erlösung'*. Neither of them carries the exact meaning of the biblical notion.

Session 21: Par. 11, Sec. 1

S: What are the main Christological heresies to be avoided, and how does one avoid them?

B: The first is Ebionitic Christology, which is explained by this syllogism: where we find a perfect appearance in life, we find God; we find perfection in Jesus Christ; therefore Jesus Christ is God. This disregards the complete otherness of God's nature. Also, it is based on man's value-judgment (for example, in Ritschl's theology). In Docetic Christology an eternal being comes to earth; this ideal being is identified with Jesus. Here there is sin against the humanity of Christ. The New Testament thinks in terms of an assertion that constantly appeals back to revelation. Its axiom: no *Weltanschauung*—only resurrection of the dead! This is the beginning for Christians. Afterwards comes logic, when we begin to witness. But all is suspended from revelation. There are only two kinds of theology: one that begins with revelation, a lot of others that begin elsewhere. The whole doctrine of the Trinity is simply an attempt to explain this beginning.

S: Can you point out any Christological heresies today?

B: Fundamentalism is docetic. Modernism is ebionitic. Bultmann combines both: his disinterest in the historical Jesus leads to Docetism; his notion that we believe only because of the faith of the Apostles is Ebionitism. In Roman Catholicism Jesus Christ as a man has disappeared, and the human factor is really Mary.

S: What do you think of the historical methods of interpreting Scripture, such as Form Criticism?

B: I think Form Criticism is helpful, useful. But I think its purpose should be to explain the documents as such, and not simply to break up the documents into small parts. At least, these must be put back together.

Session 22: Par. 11, Sec. 2

S: Are the Christological and Trinitarian dogmas not only relative but absolute authorities for the Church? Can dogma be the criterion for interpreting Scripture?

B: Dogma is an important commentary on Scripture, important because at a particular time the Church had to make this decision. It is to the Church like the advice of a father to his son. The son should listen to the father before he says he is wrong. The rightness cannot be decided in advance. We must listen to the Church Fathers in the same way. If we believe they are wrong, then we must prove it exegetically. In this sense we have in the Church a *relative* authority. We face this same question in the matter of the *Canon*. The Canon is again a decision of the Church and has relative authority. Luther himself was on the point of rejecting James, II and III John, and Revelation from the Canon! A dogma is a working hypothesis. It is not a second divine authority, not another Scripture. The question of the rejection of heresies is in principle an open question. We must rethink these heresies. Dogmatics is *never* a closed and finished work. The Church must constantly be working on dogmatics. But the dogma is never absolute, as in the Roman Catholic Church, where the dogma is from heaven! Dogma is a human work. It is the continual dogmatic task to reconsider the question of the Canon, just as it is its task to reconsider the question of the Doctrine of the Trinity. The opening of the Bible is not a *datum*, but an event! Of course, dogma is an exegetical key, but only a human key, a working hypothesis. We are not allowed to impose on Scripture the Nicene Creed, as the old dogmatists have done in some cases. The use of dogma in interpreting Scripture is a circle: we read Scripture, we read the Fathers, then we return to Scripture. I myself prefer to make use of the Fathers of Nicaea than to make use of Martin Heidegger, for instance.

S: What do you think of using the ancient symbols and creeds in a worship service?

B: The use of ancient symbols or creeds in worship is a practical question. If the congregation has been instructed and knows what it says, then all well and good. In Germany I had to recite the Nicene Creed at certain times of the year, such as Easter and Christmas. I would not forbid it, but I am a little sceptical of its use. This is a question of tact and judgment and occasion, not of principle. One thing is certain: *at first* these creeds were not meant for liturgy. If they were recited in the Church, it was as a protest against heresy.

S: What is the criterion for determining what books should be included in the Canon of Scripture?

B: In the first centuries the criterion was: Is it apostolic? Certainly lots of writings were not, and the criterion became the authenticity of the text in terms of Jesus Christ. Do we hear the Truth through these books or not? Thus the question is one of the Holy Spirit's speaking through them. If we found the manuscript of a new Gospel, the Church would be faced with the question of its canonicity. If the Holy Spirit led the Church to accept it, then it could be taken into the Canon. Another possibility would be to admit some known book, such as the Didachē or the Epistle to Diognetus. Both are good books. Should we put them in the Canon? It is possible. Or we could follow Luther and exclude James. We cannot exclude these possibilities in principle. But a general synod or council of the Church, *not* theological professors, would have to decide! The basic rule is: scripture interprets scripture!

S: What is your objection to Oscar Cullmann's concept of time?

B: Cullmann says that time existed before creation. But if time existed before creation, then what is it? Another God, another creation? Time is no quality or attribute of God unless it is God Himself.

Session 23: Par. 12, Sec. 1

S: In dealing with the relation of revelation to man on page 514, you ask the following questions: 'Will revelation, particularly this, the real revelation, reach its goal after all? Will it get at man? Will it become manifest to him?' Can we talk of 'revelation' unless it has reached its goal?

B: These questions are not assertions. In the question we can presuppose the answer, but the question must be asked. It is not self-evident. In theologising we must ask questions. I use the Socratic method for the sake of clarification.

S: Must the question of natural theology be asked?

B: Yes, naturally. We live in a Greek atmosphere in the West. We learn by asking questions. This is a basic way of thinking for us.

S: Is it not possible for God to reveal something in the world without our perceiving it?

B: What we call (regarding Scripture) 'revelation' is what comes to our perception. God can reveal Himself everywhere, in the garden, in a table, etc., but the question is: are we sure of it? And in Jesus Christ in the Bible we are sure of it. From there we know that God is everywhere. We may have glimpses outside, but I would not like to call them revelation.

S: If dogmatics must answer all questions, then is it not eristic theology?

B: Certainly, dogmatics is eristic, but this is no 'second task of theology' in the sense of apologetics (Brunner).

S: On page 515 you state that '*Pneuma Theou* or *Christou*, like *Huios Theou*, is a figure of speech.' What do you mean by 'figure of speech'?

B: We make use of some term that we know from our experience. We think we know what it means. In this sense we make use of a figure of speech. But this is not the end. We say that *pneuma* is 'wind', but it is more than wind! When we say Jesus Christ is Son of God, we mean He is the *real* Son, and what we call 'son' is only an analogy. God has entered our world, and we may use our language to try to give meaning to this event. But God is more than our words and concepts. Our vessels are earthly, whereas the content is heavenly. But the earthly character of our words does not obstruct the possibility of God's using them for His Word.

S: On page 515 you speak of the use of *pneuma* in Genesis 2.7, wherein man becomes a living being by God's breathing into his nostrils the breath of life, as the prototype of all biblical references to the divine *pneuma*. Later you speak of the *pneuma* as the possibility for conversation between God and man. Is this 'conversational relation' the same as the giving of life in Genesis 2.7?

B: This may be in the background in Genesis 2.7, but the meaning of Genesis 2.7 is more simple, namely, that through the *pneuma* man begins to be a living creature. This use of *pneuma* may be the prototype, but it is only prototype. This does not mean that the *pneuma* the prophet receives is the same.

S: In the first creation story of Genesis God creates man in the image of God, that is, in relation to God.

B: I would not say 'relation', but 'analogy'. There is something concrete to which God is related.

S: But the 'image' has been lost.

B: No, not *this* image. Only if 'image' were man's 'righteousness' would it be lost. But I think there is another interpretation.

S: Is 'breathing into man's nostrils' (second creation story) the same as 'created in the image of God' (first creation story)?

B: I do not think so. After the Fall we still breathe! Man has not changed since the Fall. He is the same man. 'God saw all things and found them very good.' Our nature is good. But the trouble is that we are sinning against our good nature. So I do not talk of a 'remnant of good' in man. Order is re-established in reconciliation. When God gives man the Holy Spirit, we become *more* than man was before the Fall. This elevation of man is the 'new birth'. We are reborn as members of Christ's Body. This is the meaning of *eikōn* in the New Testament, which is related to Genesis 1. Image in Genesis 1 means that like God, who is living but not isolated (*Elohim* denotes plurality), there is plurality in man. Man has plurality like God, who is plural. Being man means being in togetherness: man and wife. 'Living God' means 'togetherness'. This togetherness is, according to Ephesians, Christ and His Church: the *eikōn*. Image has a double meaning: God lives in togetherness within Himself, then God lives in togetherness with man, then men live in togetherness with one another. The middle term is the foundation of man's likeness to God: togetherness in relation, and proceeding out of these is an analogy. The only explanation of 'image' I will express is what I get from the *text* itself. This is the only criterion. People have said that the image of God was 'reason', 'personality', 'responsibility'; but I do not find any of these in the text. Luther and Calvin spoke of 'original righteousness', but I do not find that either. I prefer my exegesis because it binds together the Old and New Testaments: Yahweh and His People, Jesus and His Church.

S: Can we say, 'We know not *what* God is, but we know *that* He is in Christ'?

B: We have no right to make a reservation here. We also know *what* God is in Jesus Christ. It is always dangerous to make reservations, as if behind Jesus Christ there is another reality.

S: Can we say for the same reason that propositional theology is false, i.e. because this is abstract truth to which we must relate Christ?

B: Yes. Jesus Christ is the truth to which all propositions must be related, and He is more than our propositions.

S: What is 'new' in the pouring out of the Holy Spirit at Pentecost, in relation to the Spirit in the Old Testament?

B: The new thing is that the disciples now are given to 'know' and 'perceive' what was happening in Old Testament times. The understanding of God's work in the Old Testament was opened up to them. Also new is the founding and building of the Church.

Session 24: Par. 12, Sec. 2

S: Is there not a social threeness in God: real persons, centres of consciousness? Think of the New Testament, where Jesus prays to the Father, etc. Does not a love relation require two selves?

B: We cannot visualise God. His one essence does not mean that God is immovable within Himself. On the contrary! The New Testament says, 'God is love.' In the one essence of God there is togetherness; so there can be love. There are other things in God, such as authority and humility. Our minds cannot unite these, but these are in the one God. I admit a social threeness. The distinction between 'individual' and 'society' are *our* distinctions. Why not something different in God: not a *division*, although a distinction? Yes, the Son prays to the Father, and the Father hears. But this is the divine life. When we pray, we participate in this through Christ. The notion of 'distinct centres of consciousness' is rationalistic mythology. I prefer to admit the glory of God—His fulness of possibilities: past, present, future; weakness, omnipotence. All these are perfections of God, and all these mean the *one*

58

God. But God is a *living* God, not the God of the philosophers.

S: In what sense did the fourth-century theologians understand '*persona*'?

B: The Greek idea was really tritheistic: three persons just alike (like a superimposed picture). But Augustine talked in terms of 'modes of existence' or hypostases. If we have three distinct centres of consciousness, then we are not meeting the one God. You have to look around and maybe just find Jesus —or, as liberals, just the Father. Tritheism means the dissolution of the man-God relation. There is personality in God, but just one personality, not diffusion.

S: Can we not say that in God there is an 'I' and a 'Thou' and a 'He'?

B: God confronts us this way. To say that God is 'I', 'Thou', and 'He' means that He is personality. But we must avoid the neuter idea, God as an '*Etwas*' ('Something'). He is alive: an 'I', 'Thou' and 'He'. If this is admitted, then we do not need the definition of 'centres of consciousness', which is a human definition.

S: Can rational evidences and signs (as in Calvin) be used to lead men to faith, even though all is of grace, with no co-operation on man's part?

B: Do not say that man does not participate in the gift of grace! Man is given freedom by revelation to do something: human doings. The Bible speaks of co-operation. When we pray, we co-operate. This does not mean that man becomes a co-Lord. He is using the freedom given for the service of God: for prayer, research, action. 'You shall reign with me': this is the eschatological aspect of life. Here we are only in the service of God. In eschatological reality service means lordship. But no co-lordship! I agree with you up to the word 'evidences'. God can use anything. He makes use of water, wine, bread, and human beings: with their brains, sane reason in the pulpit, *sana ratio* as theologians. Here is no irrationalism. The Holy Spirit does not suppress reason; He causes rebirth of reason. But miracles are not rational evidences or convincing signs. They show the presence of the Kingdom of God, God's power over sickness, nature, and so on. They are part of *Christ's work*, but not proof for the human *ratio*. Christ is who He is; He gives no proofs. Concerning an historical proof for the resurrection, would you find this impressive? If you had historical evidence, it would not be the resurrection! This is a deed of God in Christ. I do not like Calvin on this. Can faith be confirmed by historical evidence? Here Calvin thought in terms of Roman Catholic theology. The Romans have lots of evidences as crutches, but faith is without crutches. This is not the realm of good reason: to seek rational help, crutches. What does the Bible mean by 'sign'? It is a *means of revelation*, but not rational evidence. Look at the miracles in John. Each one has a special relation to the words of Christ: proclamation. They are a sort of illustration; they make transparent what is said by Christ in the form of a deed. In words and deeds God reveals His Godhead.

S: What about Acts 1.3, which says that Christ 'presented himself alive after his passion by many proofs, appearing to them during forty days, and speaking of the kingdom of God'?

B: This has to do with the 'appearances' of Christ, not 'proofs'.

S: Are not the resurrection appearances in 1 Corinthians 15 historical evidence?

B: No. An 'evidence' would be a witness *outside* the Church. Here Paul is just showing the unity of the Church in the resurrection faith.

S: What about the story of the resurrection in Matthew 28, where the chief priests and elders pay the guards of Jesus' tomb not to reveal what had taken place?

B: Feeble evidence! Historical proof would infringe on human freedom. Faith means 'no crutches'. Faith is sustained only by the renewal of the Word of God, revelation.

S: What about the miracles that 'caused many to believe'?

B: These were persuasive, but it was not a rational persuasion as proof.

S: Theology can often be formulated in syllogisms. Does such formal logic have ultimate validity?

B: Human reason can use formal logic in theology, but the word relationship does not give it its *validity*. We can use syllogisms, but there is no ultimate validity in this kind of thinking. We may use syllogisms to the glory of God, just as a musician uses music to the glory of God. We may make use of Plato, Aristotle, Kant; we are free to use them, but we are not bound to use them. God's action is so great and manifold that we are forced to make use of various ways of thinking. We sometimes must use a syllogism, but at other times we can only use a *paradox*. It depends on what the Word of God demands. The Bible speaks so differently, with different kinds of witness, different logics. The danger is that we learn some philosophy and then begin to study theology and ask that theology follow the rules of the philosophy in our head. We can use philosophy as an instrument, but if we absolutise Hegel or Heidegger or Aristotle, then we are lost in regard to the Bible.

S: Is the use of formal logic like a parable? If so, what limits our use? Are our conclusions only opinions?

B: Our conclusions should not be opinions, but in relation to God's Word. This means a general relativisation of all philosophies. None is excluded, but none is absolute. We must learn to be liberals—as philosophers!

S: We say: 'What God is in His revelation, He is in Himself.' Since we live *post Kant*, what right do we have to make this metaphysical assertion?

B: This is not metaphysical! The Bible simply states! What does this have to do with my good friend Kant? (I like him!) Kant's critique is good for science, but he talked not of the God of the Bible, but of the idea of God. God is not within Kant's categories. The parallelism between the economic Trinity and the immanent Trinity, on the one hand, and Kant's transcendental apperception and the '*Ding an sich*' is only *formal*.

Session 25: Par. 13, Sec. 1

S: On page 3 you state that here you are concerned with the Doctrine of the Incarnation, and that the Doctrine of the Person and Work of Christ will come later in the Doctrine of Reconciliation. Does this imply a separation between the incarnation and the person and work of Christ?

B: 'Incarnation' is here used as a summary word including the whole of Christological doctrine. It is a tactical use. I had to deal with Christology even in *Prolegomena*, because Christ is the Word of God. I could not anticipate the whole Doctrine of Reconciliation, but an extract insofar as the Doctrine of Reconciliation is revelation (the prophetic office).

S: On page 8f you discuss your belief that the method of both Anselm and the Heidelberg Catechism is to speak of possibility only on the basis of reality, and you cite the famous formula: *credo ut intelligam* with obvious approval. What is the meaning of this theological method for the apologetic task of the Church? Does the Church only witness to the *fact* and leave apologetics to the Holy Spirit?

B: The best apologetics is a good dogmatics. Truth will speak for itself. You cannot convince people if you are going the wrong way. You must trust in a good way and use it. Anselm was an apologist, but he trusted in the inner strength of his way. Anselm liked to speak of the beauty of theology—a very strong evidence, but beginning with God, not general principles. In his faith, or in his faith in the object of faith, he wrote theology. Let us trust the inner witness of the Spirit.

S: Did Paul use Anselm's method in Athens?

B: Yes, I think so. The question is not where one begins. But for Paul one thing is sure: Jesus Christ. He *comes down* from Jesus Christ when he speaks of idols and Athenians, etc.—not *vice versa*. We must *think*, not just preach. The task of thinking is theology, but unlike philosophy, it is not seeking, but is explaining what has been given. Paul's speech was not a success. The Athenians laughed. But it was a witness.

S: Is there flexibility in the practice of theology?

B: Certainly! There must be freedom of thought. But the fundamental question is: are we beginning with *something given* and not seeking to find? Anselm's method and the method of the Heidelberg Catechism are not heresy, but I chose a different way because of the history of theology of the last two hundred years.

S: Did Anselm write for unbelievers? And what of Tillich's apologetic use of philosophy?

B: Indirectly, yes. But he wrote directly for the Church. Anselm began with the *prima veritas*. But Anselm believed that the best apologetic was a good commentary on faith. The truth of God cannot be proven to unbelievers, but we must live as if we believe. If a man believes, he should be able to talk about it, but not to buttress his beliefs. I am speaking of the *intellectus* of faith. You cannot just assert 'Christ! Christ!' but you must behave as someone who has learned from Christ. As a thinking creature, you must express your faith. Dogmatics must have an apologetic character: apologetic insofar as it is a good dogmatics. But we do not need a second discipline. Dogmatics must have the character of *intelligent witness*. It is a pity that Tillich is not interested in dogmatics. How many people has

Tillich converted with his philosophical arguments? I would like to know! Why not a good theology that speaks to believers and unbelievers? I cannot make a sharp distinction between believers and unbelievers. I simply do not believe it when one tells me he is an unbeliever! Probably he is fighting the truth. We should speak to such people in solidarity, as unbelievers for whom Christ died. Anselm knew who and what God is; and only then could he prove the existence of God. People have laughed at Anselm, but this is the only valid proof of God.

S: Do you think Jesus' designation of Himself as 'Son of Man' derives its meaning from the late Judaistic concept of exaltation (the 'Son of Man' coming on the clouds of heaven) or from Jesus' idea of one who comes as a servant?

B: The term 'Son of Man' has an element of exaltation (Daniel 7), but true exaltation comes through humiliation. On the cross Christ is King, the exalted Son of Man! I would not separate the elements of exaltation and humiliation. Late Judaism had only the idea of exaltation, but we should not try to correct it by saying: *not* exaltation, *but* humiliation.

S: You note two Christological theses in the New Testament: that Jesus is Christ, and that Christ is Jesus. That Christ is Jesus is the Pauline-Johannine anti-docetic view, whereas that Jesus is Christ is the anti-ebionitic view of the Synoptics. Yet later heresies grew out of the theses against these specific heresies! Can you explain this?

B: Docetism is not the same as Eutychianism. Ebionitism is not the same as the Nestorianism of the fourth century. I have in mind only a *line* of thought. In the fourth-century discussion both parties had elements of truth, one mainly from the Synoptics, the other mainly from Paul and John. Perhaps the theses are oversimplifications. But what about this riddle: that anti-docetic writers led to docetism and that anti-ebionitic writers led to ebionitism? That really is a riddle! Perhaps this is the explanation: the starting-point of Paul and John was *Christ*, a divine being. Then they said that the *Logos* become flesh. But perhaps because they had to speak so *strongly*, their thesis was overlooked and people only heard their starting-point. And the same in the case of the Synoptics. Mistakes arise when only a *part* of a sentence is heard. It happens often.

S: This question concerns the term '*kenosis*' in Philippians 2.7. The word means 'to empty' and refers to Christ's emptying Himself of His godly form and taking the form of a servant. Do not the Synoptic Gospels imply that Christ did more than *veil* His divinity?

B: The Kenotic School in German Lutheranism in the nineteenth century said that Jesus emptied Himself of His divinity and had to discover His mission and at the same time had step by step to *rediscover* His identity as Son of God. I think this is wrong. God the Son did not give up His divinity, but the *morphē tou theou*, i.e. the being of God as He knows it Himself, His glory in His heavenly form. Jesus was in this godly form, but He did not think of it as a robber who has stolen something and who now says, 'It is now mine.' Being in this form, He emptied Himself. How? Not in a loss of divinity, but in accepting to be what He was in the form of the servant of man: God's condescension, but condescension in which there was no loss of divinity. Rather, His divinity was *veiled*. God has not only His own possibility of being as He is in Himself, but He has the freedom to be God as man, with us and for us. This does not mean an alteration, but means that He can be man without ceasing to be God. God can change, but He cannot cease to be God. When Jesus was a limited being, this limitation itself was a divine act. The work of redemption is not a work alien to God. It was an act of His freedom; He did not need to redeem.

S: Would you object to someone's saying that Jesus developed self-consciousness in the Gospels?

B: Yes, because the Gospels really do not indicate it.

S: But you think it did take place?

B: That He was a child, and so forth—yes. But this is not important for the Gospels. A book on this theme would be psychological fairy tales.

S: You speak of Jesus Christ as the 'objective reality and possibility of revelation', and of the Holy Spirit as the 'subjective reality and possibility of revelation'. Do you mean to exclude man's ability to accept salvation?

B: Yes. Faith is only through the work of the Holy Spirit. That we recognise the Son of God in this man Jesus is not a recognition as man's own definite act. As an act, yes, but what we do is done on the ground of the objective and subjective realities and possibilities.

S: Is Jesus the Christ without the Church?

B: Jesus is Christ in no sphere without the Church. When we say 'Jesus Christ', we say Christ and His Body, *Totus Christus*. Christ without the Church is a spectre. The Church is not a part of His divinity, but it becomes an accessory part of divinity because God has chosen His Son to be the Saviour *for us*. The Church is elected from eternity, but Christ remains the Head (there is no such thing as a 'vicar of Christ', as in Roman Catholicism). The Church remains in a relation of grace and never becomes a necessary attribute of Christ.

S: Does the *kenosis* imply the loss of divine attributes?

B: No. These attributes cannot be lost. They mean the being of God as such in different aspects.

S: You admit that the incarnation *might* have been different (for example, docetic) if it pleased God. Does not the type of sin present in mankind *demand* the incarnation that happened?

B: We may speak of 'necessity' if we accept that God's way is right just because He chose it. It is important that we do not confuse our concept of this necessity as a necessity in itself, a system in which God is *bound* to act. This necessity of God's doing is one He has chosen, and behind it is the free grace of God, who *could* have chosen another way. We must admit that God was not bound to do what He did.

S: Athanasius says it is necessary because of man's *sin*, which God had to notice.

B: It is not good to argue from what we believe we know about sin. I based my view on Jesus Christ Himself, not on the needs of man, not even on his sin. I have tried to find the necessity of the incarnation out of the fact of the incarnation! We know sin from revelation, not from some abstract notion. Athanasius had no abstract notion either.

S: Athanasius would have said a docetic incarnation was impossible.

B: What I seek to avoid is a concept of necessity grounded elsewhere than in the reality of the incarnation. I also refuse to speak of possibility in abstract. We can talk about possibility only from the *reality*. What Athanasius and what Anselm did are *after*thoughts. Looking *back* from what we know of sin from revelation, we can say that the incarnation had to happen. No doctrine of sin can be independent. There is no system of truth in which God is a prisoner.

S: Is Anselm's God in his 'ontological argument for the existence of God' really God or an analysis of finite existence which points beyond itself?

B: I do not like either alternative. The entity that he designates 'God' is 'a greater than which cannot be conceived'. This is the 'Creator', and nothing could be greater than the Creator. God is witnessed to in the Christian revelation. Anselm addressed himself to believers—to his monks, not to unbelievers. Descartes and his followers did not understand the deep meaning of Anselm.

S: On page 34 you state the following: 'There is—amid the complete dissimilarity of divine and non-divine—a similarity between the eternal Word of God and the world created by this Word, but also and still more a similarity between the eternal, natural, only-begotten Son and those who are through Him God's adopted sons, who by grace are His children.' What is the similarity? If it is the outward form, then would this not be docetism?

B: We are speaking of analogy: similarity within dissimilarity. In theology, analogy is where God chooses to act and to reveal Himself among us in created forms. Then what happens? These created forms as such are transformed. They remain the forms, which means they remain dissimilar, but because God *chooses* them, they become analogous to the Creator: similar and yet dissimilar. This is not *analogia entis*, but *analogia fidei* or *relationis* or *actionis*, or *benevolentia Dei*. We are human children of a human father. Then God chooses to be our Father by becoming a Brother to us. In this way God gives the word 'Father' a new meaning. It is dissimilar to what our child-father relation is, but because God has chosen to become our Father, there is similarity. The new meaning transcends our meaning. This is the *real* meaning of fatherhood, for the Original Father and the Original Son is God.

S: To what extent is revelation in accord with the world and to what extent is it an exception to the worldly?

B: God's incarnation happens in connexion with worldly things. The New Testament emphasises this in many ways, for instance, in the miracle stories in which Jesus heals sickness or calms a storm on the sea and in the stories of the resurrection which speak of Jesus' body and of His eating fish. To this extent, revelation does not infringe on the nature of the cosmos. Even the miracle of our conversion happens in our *mind*; our brain and blood are involved. Miracles *perhaps* could even be explained as happenings of natural law by means of psychology, theosophy, etc. But then these things are not understood as miracles. What is significant in miracle is that it is a *doing of God*. Faith is as much a miracle as the Virgin Birth. Both in the Bible are doings of God and thus are mystery.

S: When you speak of Christ as 'human' and 'divine', are these dimensions?

B: If you wish, but do not divide them, because the whole is divine and not-divine. What is not divine becomes divine. In Christ there is always togetherness of God and man. Do not separate the two natures.

S: On page 40 you say that Jesus Christ 'was also flesh. Of course, as His humanity, it became a different thing from ours, for sin, man's strife with God, could not find any place in Him.' Does 'it' refer to Jesus' humanity or flesh?

B: Flesh. Jesus' humanity and flesh are identical. Both are different from ours because of His sinlessness. Sin could not find any place in His flesh (Romans 8). Paul says He had to fight sin in the flesh, but sin is overwhelmed.

Session 27: Par. 14, Sec. 1

S: This question concerns the assertion of H. J. Kraus in his article on 'Das Problem der Heilsgeschichte in der *Kirchlichen Dogmatik*' in *Antwort*, that your use of terms like '*Urgeschichte*' and '*Heilsgeschichte*' has changed a great deal during the years between the *Römerbrief* and the *Church Dogmatics*. Do you agree?

B: Yes, I agree with his explanation that I had to purify these terms before I could use them again. My use depended upon the time and the opponents. Against Bultmann I later had to insist on a *Heilsgeschichte*. Everything depends on the context. This applies to the use of *Übergeschichte* in Volume II, Part 1; it simply means that eternity embraces our time. This is the problem of words. Sometimes words used in a bad context can be baptised and used again. The Anglo-Saxon mind can accept this better than the French, who complain when a word is not used entirely consistently. Consistency is good, but it may indicate poverty. A new day may call for a new use of the word.

S: Has '*Heilsgeschichte*' been baptised yet? Reinhold Niebuhr says Oscar Cullmann makes a God of 'time'.

B: I am not so sure that Niebuhr is wrong. Cullmann does!

S: Cullmann sees time and *Heilsgeschichte* as a horizontal line without beginning and without end, but with Christ as the mid-point. Revelation is a point in history. You have attempted to overcome this by seeing Christ in Old Testament prophecy, etc. But is there not a difficulty between 'once-for-all' and your idea that Christ is before and after the revelation of the years A.D. 1-30?

B: *Eph' hapax* does not mean once, but once-*for-all*. Christ was as such and always will be. There is only an apparent contradiction. What happened once-for-all is not abstract and isolated singularity—a single event, yes, but not limited by the restriction of its present. Its present is also past and future. *Chronos* is our clock time. *Kairos* is the time of God coming into our time (the use of *kairos* in the New Testament is *theological*, not simply philological).

S: When I die, does created and creation time cease?

B: When you die, your time is over. Insofar as God comes into your life and saves you, your created time is saved.

S: How should the words '*nicht wiederholen konnte*' on page 57, line 10, of the German text be interpreted? The translation on page 51 of the English edition reads as follows: 'Just as man's existence became something new and different altogether, because God's Son assumed it and took it over into unity with His God-existence, just as by the eternal Word becoming flesh the flesh *was able not to repeat* Adam's sin, so time, by becoming the time of Jesus Christ, although it belonged to our time, the lost time, became a different, a new time.'

B: The English translation here is a catastrophe! '*Non posse peccare*' ('not able to sin') is the right meaning. Heinrich Vogel says that the human nature taken by Christ was a 'holy' flesh. I say no. It is *our* flesh, but if Christ takes on our flesh, then a sanctification of the flesh takes place, and then the man in Christ cannot sin. But the sinlessness of Christ is a *deed*, not a quality.

S: How should we interpret '*posse non peccare*' and '*non posse peccare*' in the life of Christ?

68

B: '*Non posse peccare*' is a deed of God, not a quality. When this is understood, then you can speak of volition. There is a real will in this deed. Temptation was very real for Jesus, but a temptation that could not be followed by a new 'Fall', because now God has chosen to be man. The repetition of Genesis 3 is impossible. Nevertheless, the reality of a sanctified life was a *fight*, not just a being. Jesus had *to obey*. But it was a fight that could not have another result.

S: Can '*non posse peccare*' become a possibility for us in this life?

B: Yes, *in our union with Christ* it is true for us. We can sin only far away from Christ, but not in and with Him. Sin is an impossible possibility. It is made impossible for us by Christ. If we sin, we do the impossible. It is an *ontological* impossibility (even if Berkouwer does not like it!). In Genesis 3 the *serpent* is the impossible.

S: You acknowledge a human side of *Heilsgeschichte*. What is the function of archaeological research in the Church, for instance, in this connexion?

B: I do not like books that try to prove the rightness of the Bible by archaeological research, but the results of this research are an important help in understanding the biblical witness to Christ. However, no historical research can help us *prove* God's revelation as reality. Historical research will never be an *approach* to the Word of God.

S: On page 65 you state that the confession of the miracle 'God reveals Himself' does not imply a blind credence in all the miracle stories related in the Bible. On what grounds do we accept miracles?

B: I only say that we do not have to accept all the miracles *in globo*. I did not speak of excluding any miracle. There is *one* great miracle that is reflected in the miracles. It is not the miracle*s* as such that count, but *the* miracle that is reflected in them. We cannot reason: the Bible tells us the truth; the Bible tells us of miracles; therefore we must accept the miracles. No, the Bible tells us of *the* miracle of revelation. Perhaps there are miracles that are in the present time not enlightening for us, but may be in another time. I would go between a general acceptance and a general refusal. We do not believe in miracles, but in God. No miracle can be accepted on *historical* grounds and therefore cannot be refused on these grounds.

PART III

Concerning Several of Karl Barth's Monographs

A. *Church and State**

S: In the Synoptic Gospels is there a negative connexion between Church and State? The Reformers and you both use the trial account of The Gospel of John, in which Jesus tells Pilate that he would have no power over Him if it were not given from above. In the Synoptics' account of the trial, Jesus refuses to answer at all. Here there seems to be a *lack* of connexion between Church and State.

B: John could be a commentary here on the Synoptics. It is true that in the Synoptics Jesus remains silent, but I do not think this account is in conflict with John's or that it means there is a 'negative connexion'. After all, in the Synoptics the two orders (Church and State) are established; they work in different ways, but together, and the result is the same. Why not understand John as an exposition of this relationship? The Synoptics do not say 'power from above', but they presuppose this power. Barabbas is also in the Synoptics, and this is very important. Pilate arranges his freedom, thus functioning as *exsecutor novi testamenti*!

S: But is there a lack of connexion?

B: In some sense, as in John. But *implicitly* the connexion even in the Synoptics is a *positive* one.

S: Many people make a big difference between the trial of Jesus in John and in the Synoptics.

B: There is just a difference of *emphasis*. The real duty of Pilate is shown in both. The decision of Pilate himself is what is important; he falls short of his duty. There is no real difference in *essence*.

S: Is the relation between Pilate and Jesus *normative* for the relation between Church and State, i.e. the State's miscarriage of justice? Is this case normative or an exception?

* The title of G. Ronald Howe's English translation of *Rechtfertigung und Recht* (*Justification and Justice*), Heft 1, *Theologische Studien*, 1938. Published by the S.C.M. Press, London, 1939. Republished in *Community, State and Church*, Doubleday and Co., Garden City, New York, 1960.

B: The normality is that even an evil State cannot escape doing God's will, that is, something good. 'The blood of the martyrs is the seed of the Church!' The suffering of Christians at the hands of the State is many times a strengthening of the Church. Christians in the Communist East Zone tell me they live in a certain joy because they are advancing in faith under persecution. But we cannot build the idea of the relation of Church and State on this, because then the Church would expect nothing but persecution and would invite persecution and would ask Christians to deny their duties to the State. Ignatius *asked* for the lions! Well, good! But we need not do this. It is not the Christian's duty to ask for lions!

S: Then, is not the relation of Jesus and Pilate an exception rather than a norm?

B: Yes, I agree.

S: I do not understand your treatment of this section. Why must Pilate free Barabbas, say Jesus is innocent, and so forth?

B: The point is that Pilate acts according to political expediency and against the duty of the State; and yet he cannot but serve the will of God.

S: Could we say that Pilate *has* to be there for the atonement?

B: I do not like the word 'has'. Pilate did the *wrong* thing, but even so, he did it in the service of God. This is an example of how the political order remains a divine order even if the representative fails to do his duty.

S: Why did you choose the confrontation between Jesus and Pilate as the beginning for this monograph?

B: This is a literary question. I had Karl Ludwig Schmidt's article, 'Das Gegenüber von Kirche und Staat in der Gemeinde des Neuen Testaments', before me, and I did not like the way he just left Jesus and Pilate in confrontation. Then, too, the Reformers use this text in treating the Church-State problem. Finally, I do not know another place in the New Testament where issues are more sharply drawn and answered.

S: I find a difference in the idea of demons and the State in the second section of this monograph, where you deal with Romans 13, and that of the *Church Dogmatics*, Volume III, Part 3. Are all *exousiai* demonic forces, or are some good angels?

B: I was afraid you would discover this difference! Now I feel we must not distinguish between the different *names* of the powers. All of these can be used in a good sense as angels of

God, but there is also a world of demons and the *same names* are used for them. But there is no connexion between the good and the bad. There is no fall of angels! I do not deny the existence of the bad, but they are hypostases of *das Nichtige*. God did not create demons. Sin and demons are 'impossible possibilities'! They exist in a reality without possibility. This is my present understanding, as developed in Volume III, Part 3.

S: Why this shift?

B: I have studied the whole question of angels in the Old and New Testaments. When angels are spoken of, they are on the right side, accompanying the great deeds of God. There is no relation between the 'heavenly armies' of the Old Testament and the world of rebellion against God. Satan and his forces are another kind of beings in contrast with God and His angels. Angels announce the will of God. They appear, for example, at the annunciation and the resurrection. Only in Romans 13 do I find *exousiai* in the service of God. But there is no use of them as an order of God parallel to the angelic order.

S: In Job, Satan is called 'son of God'.

B: I have some trouble, I will admit. Even in the New Testament these powers are 'above', 'in heaven'. But even their 'heaven' must be a lie! The notion of the fall of angels in Jude and II Peter—I do not like this! But I cannot be too sure. The question may be even more complicated than I have seen it, even in III.3. What *is* clear is that Christ has *subjected* all these powers under Himself. We must no longer fear them. 'I saw Satan *fall* from heaven . . .'—that is my point! We must have a clear and short look at demonology, but that is enough. I have experienced too much of this abysmal side of life from the Germans, and if you look too much at it, you fall under the *power* of the demons!

S: Oscar Cullmann's article on the most recent discussion of the *exousiai* in Romans 13.1 states that most German New Testament scholars demythologise the demonic powers. Can we consider *exousiai* both as demonic forces and human forces?

B: When a State goes from good to bad, then it passes from angelic to demonic powers.

S: Can we say with Hans von Campenhausen that we really do not need the concept of demons any more?

B: Yes, I think so. Demonic action has no ontology. Even good angels have no ontology in the Bible! In the Bible angels are only some special appearance of God's own action. They are not God, but they belong to His action. They have no separate ontology.

S: Are *exousiai* angelic powers?

B: No, I think not. I do not like the negative accent that falls on the State when we think of its being demonised. In Romans 13 *'exousiai'* refers to the State (Rome) according to my view.

S: If both Church and State have the same model and goal (the 'New Jerusalem'), must they not be more closely connected? Can the State not learn from the Church that justification is the basis of justice? Can the State be neutral to truth?

B: The State as such is neutral, but the men who make up the State are not neutral. The order of the State is neutral. The meaning of the State is seen in its function to make room for the Church. Thus the State has an *inclination* toward the Church. Christ is the centre of both.

S: Does the State not know its Lord? Or does it not know true justice?

B: The State is based on the *power*, not the knowledge, of Christ. The Church is based on the knowledge of Christ. *Statesmen* can learn that justification is the basis of justice, but not the State, which is an order as such. *Ontologically* the Church is not to be separated from the State. Luther thought of the State as a purely external order separated from the spiritual order. I say the State has a relation to the spiritual order. Paul calls rulers 'deacons'.

S: But you separate man and office, whereas Luther thought of the man as the State. Your State seems abstract.

B: That is difficult to answer. What we call 'State' would be a revolution for Luther. He has no idea of a State in which every man is responsible.

Session 2: Section 4

S: What is the relation of the State to creation and reconciliation? Is the State an order of creation or under Christ? Is it under the general providence of God?

B: The State is no order of creation because of sin. It is a restraint of sin, which is due to the Fall of humanity. There is no *general* governing by providence. The world is ruled by God in Jesus Christ. There is but *one* order, that of God in Jesus

Christ! Jesus has lived and died in the disorder of this world and has re-established the order of creation (also more than that, of course!). There is now only an order of reconciliation or re-established creation.

S: Are States a fallen part of creation?

B: No. An order of God cannot fall. Man may abuse God's order, but the order does not become disorder. Man is in disorder. By 'order' I mean '*ordinatio*': not something static, but the living will of God among humanity, which has fallen, but not without God's allowing the Fall to happen.

S: In the reconciliation in Christ has the State been reconciled with God?

B: No, *man* has been reconciled, not the State.

S: What is the relation of the State to God's election?

B: That is difficult to say. The object of election is Jesus Christ, the Church, and the individual. God has chosen the Church and humanity, but this has no *direct* relation to the State. The State is a means of the execution of God's election; it may serve God.

S: How do you ground Romans 13 Christologically?

B: Paul speaks of God's having instituted *exousiai* in Romans 12, 13, and 14. Do you think he would speak of *exousiai* differently in Chapter 13 than in Chapters 12 and 14, where he definitely connects them with God in Jesus Christ? Has Paul lost his Christological understanding of God here? I do not think so. And I do not need the angels here!

S: What is the relation of divine justice to human law? I have a feeling that human law comes off short in your presentation.

B: Eternal justice is one: that of Jesus Christ. Over against this, we have the idea of general human rights. Even in the Church we have '*Kirchenrecht*'. In the State we have '*politische Recht*'. We have moral standards, written and unwritten. The result of all these enterprises is 'law'. All law—moral, ecclesiastical, and political—is human law, an attempt to understand divine justice in terms of human rules. No human law is identical with God's own justice, but is an attempt to interpret it. Divine law is the *criterion* for human law. But no law can *replace* the law of God. Human law is only man's attempt to fulfil his responsibility. Man must remain free and open for corrections, for the possibility of better law. Life in the human

74

realm must be life prepared to establish laws, but free for correction.

S: Are 'right' and 'law' the same thing?

B: No. Law is an attempt to establish what is right. For me *'Gerechtigkeit'* means 'rightfulness', which is stronger than 'righteousness'.

S: Why did you not use *'Gesetz'*?

B: *'Gesetz'* may and must be used in speaking of the *result* of political action. The result is always *'Gesetz'*.

S: Are men aware of God's law when legislating?

B: Often it is unconscious, especially in the moral realm. But in the ecclesiastical and political realms it is not unconscious, but must become conscious.

S: What about the Law of Hammurabi?

B: God was not dead at the time of Hammurabi! God is never *'menschenlos'* (without man), although we say that man is *'gottlos'* (Godless). Hammurabi was an exponent of the order of God, as Luther always said: it is so even among the Turks.

S: Then there is a natural theology or law?

B: No. There is neither natural theology nor natural law, but the omnipotence of God who is acting in all of history. Humanity is never without traces of this action, but there is no natural law which reveals itself as self-evident truth.

S: Both *'Recht'* and *'exousia'* are used in connexion with the State. What is the relation between justice and power, *Recht* and *exousia*?

B: The essence of the State is not power (*exousia*) but the establishment of justice (*Recht*). However, the particular form of this establishment is that the State imposes justice by power. Moral law cannot be enforced by power, nor can ecclesiastical law. But State law *must* be enforced by power. The right of the State is finally identical with the right in the realm of responsibility to God, but in the State it must be enforced. The worst sinner must pay taxes! Not power for power's sake; that is anarchy, tyranny. Power should only be a means of the establishment of right or justice.

S: Must you be subjected to the power before you consider whether it is just or not?

B: Both go together.

S: What is a 'totalitarian oath'?

B: This is an *unconditional* oath. I had in mind the oath

demanded in Germany by Adolf Hitler. All officials had to pledge an oath to the person of Hitler. One may take an oath on a constitution, but not to a Fuehrer! Also, an oath of 'loyalty' is different from one of 'obedience'. Loyalty may be interpreted.

S: What criteria may be used in deciding whether or not to try to overthrow an unjust government? I think, for instance, of the plot against Hitler in which Dietrich Bonhoeffer was involved.

B: That is a big question. You mention Bonhoeffer. This was a big question for Christians in Nazi Germany and may become one for others. Let me propose three *relative* criteria (not *absolute*; that is only the living God in His commandment!): (1) A government may be overthrown (that is, an attempt may be made) if its behaviour shows such a measure of injustice and inhumanity that the point is reached where you have the conviction that this government can no longer exist. This is dangerous, for you must ask yourself: are you *sure* that the government is intolerable? Perhaps it is wise to wait a little. If you are sure (before God!) then you may think of revolution, but perhaps not yet attempt it. (2) An attempt to overthrow the government may only be made if *all* other means of remedying the situation have been exhausted. There may be other means of accomplishing your purpose. You may find ways to replace bad men or to change their position. If you are sure all ways are exhausted, then you may think of revolution. (3) If you are sure revolution must come, then you must still ask yourself this question: have you a *real* opportunity to better the situation? Revolution is not so difficult, but what will you do the next day? If you are not sure that good can come of it, then do not do it. There have been too many revolutions in which the first and second conditions have been met, but not the third. This was my reservation about the plot to overthrow Hitler. Bonhoeffer and his friends were not clear about what would happen afterwards. Plans were not concrete for afterwards. There was not a clear positive position. Negative, yes. But clear vision on practical possibilities was lacking. They were dreamers. Now if you are sure on all *three* points, then you must *pray* and ask God if He is also of the same mind. Without God's will, the best intention of man cannot be realised. But here we are back to the *absolute* criterion.

S: What would be the criterion for your first criterion?

B: Look at Romans 13, where it says that the task of the State is to protect good men and to suppress bad men. If these conditions are *reversed*, if the State represents power for power's sake, then the point may be reached where we may say that the men at the head of the government (not the order of government itself) must be overthrown.

S: Can you think of a revolution that fulfilled all three criteria?

B: Perhaps the American Revolution.

S: If Thomas Jefferson had read the *Church Dogmatics* and *Church and State* before he wrote *The Declaration of Independence*, how do you think he would have opened this text?

B: That is difficult to answer, but I will try. You want a Christian dogmatic statement. I will put myself in Jefferson's place and try to improve his statement as follows: *We hold these truths to be evident* (not 'self-evident', for that smacks of natural theology! Using 'evident', the Christian will think 'evident from the will of God' and the non-Christian will interpret it to mean 'self-evident'), *that all men are created* (not 'equal'; that's too formal; what is meant by 'equal'?) *in togetherness and mutual responsibility* ('togetherness' means that man belongs with man and is responsible to man; then they are related to each other, and then equality is a *living* thing, something that can be said only of *men*), *that they are endowed by their Creator with freedom of life within the bounds of a rightfully established common order.* I do not like the notion of individual rights, with the idea that the State must protect the right of individuals. The State must protect the *freedom* (not 'liberty', which is a strange Latin word) of man, which means also responsibility. Freedom and responsibility are not opposed, but go together. Freedom of life cannot be described in terms of individual existence, but of *community* (and I do not mean a crowd of thieves and murderers!). The State has to protect men who are constituted by togetherness and responsibility within these bounds.

B. *The Christian Community and the Civil Community**

Session 1: Sections 1-13

B (introductory remarks): I hope you have seen progress in

---

* The title of Stanley Godman's English translation of *Christengemeinde und Bürgergemeinde*, Heft 20, *Theologische Studien*, 1946. Published by the S.C.M. Press in *Against the Stream*, London, 1954. Republished in *Community, State and Church*, Doubleday and Co., Garden City, New York, 1960.

this writing over *Church and State*: more clear, more understandable. But let us hear the questions.

S: At the end of section 5 you speak of the Christian community as an inner circle within the wider circle of the civil community. That is, you use the notion of two concentric circles. Would not the scriptural notion of the 'leaven in the loaf' be a better description?

B: In the parable dealing with 'leaven in the loaf' the Kingdom of God and the world are compared. It seems to me that it is wise to avoid an all-too-fast equation between Church and Kingdom, and State and world. The Church must proclaim the Kingdom; the State is an ordinance within the world. However, we cannot identify these. But you ask if we may not use the analogy, and I say it could be done. Every figure and parable is somewhat misleading and has its weakness. What we miss in the figure of the concentric circles is the dynamic relation between the inner and outer circles. The inner circle should have many *arrows* pointing outward—showing that it is distinguished but not separated (like the Chalcedonian formula!). If I prefer this figure, it is because of its ability to show that the centre of the two communities or ordinances is identical, that centre being Jesus Christ. The biblical parable would not show this. A parable cannot be shown, only told. Thus a geometric figure has certain advantages in this case. With this figure the idea of the 'two kingdoms' is overthrown.

S: By 'Christian community' and 'civil community' do you mean two institutions or the men who are in them?

B: I do not like the term 'institution' and prefer 'God's order'. The communities are within certain orders. Those who make up the communities (and for the Christian community I prefer the word '*Gemeinde*' to '*Kirche*', because *Gemeinde* means togetherness) are called to obey. The Lordship of Christ works in the Christian community as *free* obedience. In the State, obedience is also asked, but the State can ask for obedience with no question of freedom. But even in the State, if obedience is only legal and outward, this is not good. The State also needs action as free responsibility, but the State cannot *ask* for citizens to be free. The State lives out of what the Church can say.

S: If the State is serving God in perversity, is revolution in order?

B: There may be revolution in obedience to God's order: an obedience in compliance to civic duty and as such not against God. But then revolution would not be against, but *for* the State. Here there is no question of overthrowing the *State*, but only the present rulers in order to institute better government.

S: Are you more positive about revolution than Calvin?

B: I learned something from Calvin. Calvin wanted to avoid an insurrection of the whole population, but would delegate authority to make revolution to the hierarchy. Calvin was conservative, but he saw that there can be no *absolute* conservatism. He asked obedience until the last possibility is reached, but he recognised that the time may come when there must be revolution.

S: 'Ordinances' seems too static a concept for the notion of the Lordship of Christ. Christ's activity is *virile* and must be recognised in the State as well as the Church.

B: Christ is *known* as Lord only in the Church, so only Christians know what it means to be obedient to Him. But the same Christ also governs without the Church. This is what Paul means in Colossians 1, when he says that Christ is above all. That is the presupposition for Christian action in the civil community: that Christ is also there.

S: How much is the Christian community concerned with *success* in politics? Should Christians be willing to get their hands dirty?

B: We *must* hope for success, but we must never come to the point of *wanting* to get our hands dirty. We cannot want to sin. According to Lutheran politics, I have to sin and ask for forgiveness! Christians should not employ an evil means for a good end. If I as a Christian am convinced that something must be done, then I must do it, and it will not be dirty. During the war I was asked by some people in the Netherlands, who were in difficulty with the occupying Germans and felt at times compelled to lie, if their action was right. I answered: Do it—but not with a bad conscience. If you have a bad conscience, then do not do it. But if you must lie in the name of justice (*iustitia*), then do it. No dirty hands here!

S: What about politics connected with the American elections?

B: This is a difficult problem. A Christian must ask himself to what degree he will go into politics. But in any case, he must not go into politics with the express idea of getting dirty hands.

S: Can one go against such a command as 'Thou shalt not kill'?

B: We must distinguish between murder and killing. Think of the Hitler situation, for instance. 'You shall not *murder*' is the right translation, not 'you shall not kill.' A soldier or a policeman is not a murderer. One might have to kill. In the Old Testament there are many killings for God's sake. And even in the New Testament we have the saying, 'Those who take the sword will be killed by the sword.' Certainly this presupposition is not that of the Church, but is that of the State. The State presupposes coercion. Think of yourself as a policeman or a soldier in the army. We must choose the best possibility and not hesitate, but act with a good conscience. The Communist acts either by following a system of ideas (Marxism) where he finds out the right thing to do and feels protected by the system or by finding out the right moment of history (the *Kairos*). But the Christian has *no system*. A Christian lives *before God*—not before a God who has no face, but the triune God revealed in Jesus Christ. So he is not dependent on a system. We can only be obedient in relation to God. We obey God, not a system. The end does not justify the means. If it is God who is asking me to act in a certain situation, then *God* justifies the means. Sure, the two may look the same, but we must risk this. We cannot help it because we are men.

Session 2: Sections 14-27

S: In section 14 you state that there is an analogical relation between the State and the Kingdom of God. What about the many historical differences in the understanding of this analogy? For instance, Eusebius thought the State should be a monarchy, the Puritans thought it should be a democracy, etc.

B: The question is whether Eusebius is right. One decision cannot be regarded as correct for the whole. If we regard democracy as better in respect to individual responsibility, then Eusebius' idea must go. But Eusebius' 'analogy' is more than an analogy. He should not have thought of God, but of God in Jesus Christ. The one God in Jesus Christ, who became our brother, is closer to the democratic idea. The idea of God's sovereignty is not exclusively Puritan. In Jesus Christ we are all brothers; this is the point that tends toward democracy.

Democracy is not in the middle between anarchy and tyranny, but is *above* both, above this dichotomy. Anarchy and tyranny are two sides of the same thing. There are certain types of government that cannot be condoned by the Christian: fascism, for instance. There is no analogy between fascism and the Kingdom of God. Fascism is pure *potentia*.

S: Would you explain why 'democracy' is analogous to the relation of Jesus and His disciples?

B: Jesus is Head of His disciples and made them brothers. Brotherhood is close to the democratic idea. I must confess I do not like the term 'democracy'; there should be a better term. Democracy means not only *for* the people but *through* the people. The latter rules out the possibility of the 'enlightened despot'.

S: Does not Romans 12.19 ('Beloved, never avenge yourselves, but leave it to the wrath of God . . .') contradict what you say in section 26 about the 'anger of God' justifying violent solutions of conflicts in the political community?

B: What do you think of Peter's attitude toward Ananias and Sapphira in Acts 5, or of Paul's attitude toward the man in Corinth who committed incest? Certainly the utmost must be done to have peace, but not peace *at all costs*. Even a Mennonite must be glad to have a policeman for protection. I think we must do what we can for peace, but this does not mean we must be pacifists. Pacifism is an absolutism (like all 'isms'). We obey *God*, not a principle or idea. So we must leave open *for the last resort* the possibility of war. Speaking *practically*, during World War II I had Christian friends in Germany, but to protect Switzerland from National Socialism I had to join the army and guard a bridge over the River Rhine, which separated the two countries. If one of my Christian friends had tried to blow up the bridge, I would have had to shoot.

Session 3: Sections 28-35

S: How do we move from our theological affirmations to political implications, that is, to definite political decisions?

B: Do you have an answer?

S: I would rather not try. I think the affirmations would yield ideals or principles, like the brotherhood of man, for instance.

B: Do you think of a Christian giving a Christian foreign policy to the United States?

S: Yes.

B: In a political situation the Christian must not only ask himself about the practical demands of this or that party. We do not decide on principles, but on conclusions. What spirit or attitude lies behind the possible positions? On the basis of criteria (the twelve I outlined, for instance) we ask: Is a fight for or against man, or is it for a principle only, or is it perhaps a fight about personal rights? Can we not discern the attitudes? Is the fight between East and West today over humanity—or is it not over an idea or a way of life? Then we move to the next criterion: Is it for the sake of human rights, for the sake of human community, etc.? To take a stand from a Christian point, one must *study*. Then one must discern the spirits! There are always two different spirits, although the difference is relative. It is not as if the Holy Spirit were on one side and the devil on the other! But the relative difference is important. There is no heaven and hell in politics, no light and darkness, but perhaps there is more light on one side. Of course, the Christian might have to take a third stand.

S: What is the difference between a 'principle' and a 'criterion'?

B: A criterion is not a point of a programme. If I say 'humanity', what this means must be found in the *concrete* situation. All criteria are *approximations*. Principles are fixed. You cannot live by principles. Life is not a field of the application of certain aprioris, but a realm where aprioris must be found out. Criteria can only give directions. The Christian must be awake and work to discover the spirits, and then make his decision in faith. Perhaps you have to oppose your Christian brethren. A *decision* made at a certain moment may be more important than the most important Christian dogma!

S: Is the third way you mentioned a 'way out'?

B: No, never a way out of a mess. The third way may take the way of a minority decision.

S: Is not obedience more characteristic of discipleship than trust (faith)?

B: The two cannot be separated. There is no trust without obedience. For Calvin you cannot separate justification and sanctification. For the Lutherans, I am not sure. For Lutherans the idea of individual responsibility is lacking. The State does the acting, and individuals must obey the State.

S: Would you say that Hitler could not have arisen in a Calvinist country?

B: Calvinism is not a sure way of keeping out the devil! But I think the opposition would have come sooner.

S: Is it possible for non-Christians to come to the same political conclusions as Christians?

B: Why not? Non-Christians are under the government of Jesus Christ, perhaps against their will and without knowing it. A non-Christian might be applying Christian criteria—and perhaps sooner than Christians. Think of the time of the Enlightenment in Europe or the time of slavery in the United States, or think of the fight for the rights of labour or the rights of women. The Church often was on the wrong side in these fights. We must confess it.

S: How, then, do we avoid natural theology?

B: If God in Christ is governing the world, then we need no natural law. We are bound to God's Word in the Church, but God is not bound. Why should God not speak to Hammurabi? God even uses men who are adhering to principles. We need the Christian point of view even to see *approximately* what God is doing in history. We cannot read history from the viewpoint of natural law or a *Weltanschauung*.

S: Can a State be both good and evil?

B: The State is always both good and evil—just like the Church, for that matter.

S: Is God's Lordship over the State limited?

B: No, it is not limited, only *hidden*. We are awaiting the revelation of God's Lordship. It is hidden not only in the State, but also in the Church! Sometimes God's work in the world is clearer than His work in the Church!

S: May the Church be concerned for its own unity when a political decision would bring division?

B: We may *have* to divide—not to destroy the unity of the Church, but to find a new form of unity for the Church. We might have to separate to find our unity on a higher level. Look at the division of the churches over the slavery question in the United States. Out of this perhaps they will find a new unity that is better than the old one. There will always be struggle between the 'true Church' and the institution.

S: I am thinking of the 'Body of Christ'.

B: Look at the situation that developed in the Church at

Corinth. What happened there (the divisions) was dangerous, but not so dangerous that it could not be healed by Paul. Life is always dangerous. You cannot define 'Body' apart from its members. The contrast between individuals and community is a modern contrast, not one of the New Testament. There is only a community of individuals. The New Testament concept of 'Body' is above this contrast. The ideal situation would be for the whole Body to act in common in the State, but even in the Church this sort of unity is not visible. Think of the important decisions within the inner life of the Church. Would there have been any Reformation if the Reformers had waited for the whole Body to act? This also applies in regard to the State. Someone has to spring forward as an officer before his men, and he asks others to follow. But he does it as a part of the Church, not as an individual. His is no 'individual' witness, but the witness of a *member of Christ's Body*. He must dare to act. Without risk there is no life. Our unity is in Christ.

S: How do we make the catholic Christian Church a reality?

B: *Christ* makes the Church 'Christian', not we. The Church is made up of those who live in Christ. The Church is 'catholic' where every member understands himself as living in the Body of Christ. Then he lives not individually but with brethren. We have many different churches today. That is true. But suppose in each church there are people living and thinking in relation to Christ. Do you not think there will be a similar 'community' in reference to the State, a kind of 'Christian common sense' among these people when they are dealing with political matters? We are together in Christ. What we have to find out is *how* we are together. Let us cultivate the Ecumenical Movement. The life of the Church is the life of Jesus Christ Himself. If Christ is preached in the churches, the togetherness will be seen. We must seek a way to avoid 'institutional' questions. Perhaps the time is not so far away that even in the Roman Catholic Church Christ will be seen as the unity of the Church. Let them have their pope and Mary and institution. It is not so important if they from their side and we from ours see our unity in Christ.

S: Would you sanction a Methodist political party or a Presbyterian political party?

B: Heavens no!

84

S: Would you oppose so-called 'Christian political parties' already in existence?

B: Certainly!

S: Does the phrase 'class-conditioned outlook and morality' apply to all Christians under the Word of God?

B: Christians under the Word of God should not be 'class-conditioned', etc. No 'principles'! Therefore no bourgeoisie church, no socialist church. Let the Church be the Church—its own light.

C. *The Teaching of the Church Regarding Baptism**

Session 1: Sections I-III

S: Would you agree with the Anglican Prayer Book, which states that baptismal water is 'sanctified for the mystical washing away of sin'?

B: 'Sanctify us to recognise in this water the mystical washing away of sin' would be my formulation. In the New Testament sanctification is applied to persons, not to things (such as water). Perhaps we could speak of a sanctification of the whole *action* of Baptism, but not of water as such. Water as such is a means, but it is not sanctified.

S: Sanctification means 'to set apart' for a special use.

B: The *use* of water is sanctified, but not the *water*.

S: What does the New Testament mean when it says Jesus 'blessed' bread?

B: That is not exactly the same. Jesus blessed bread in the *act of communion*. Eating together was very important then. Jesus blessed the bread, but the object of the blessing was the people sharing His communion. No particular quality was given to the bread. Blessing is a strong form of prayer. Ordinary prayer is addressed only to God; a blessing is addressed to others with the assurance that the prayer will be answered. This kind of blessing is a symbol of something I do, such as addressing myself to God and including another.

S: What about the notion of 'holy places' in the Old Testament?

---

* The title of Ernest A. Payne's English translation of *Die kirchliche Lehre von der Taufe*, Heft 14, *Theologische Studien*, 1943. Published by the S.C.M. Press, London, 1948. Readers are reminded that Professor Barth's full doctrine of Baptism and the Lord's Supper is still to come in Volume IV, Part 4, of the *Church Dogmatics* and that his thinking on this subject has not remained static.

B: 'Holy places' are places at which holiness can be obtained. There is no abstract idea of 'holy places' in the Old Testament, only *concrete* places.

S: Oscar Cullmann says that Baptism and the Lord's Supper make us contemporary with the redemption in Christ, whereas the New Testament makes us contemporary with the apostolic witness to Christ. Do you agree with this?

B: I cannot make this distinction. 'He that hears you hears me.' If one hears the apostolic witness and is contemporary, then he is contemporary with Christ's redemption. Sacraments do not play such a great role in the New Testament as they do in the brains of many theologians. If Cullmann were right, then this would be more important in the New Testament.

S: Do sacraments have the power to give an immediate relation to Jesus Christ, a power that reading the Bible does not?

B: What do you mean?

S: Scripture *witnesses* to the presence of Christ. In the life of the Church, community with Christ is *felt* in the Lord's Supper. Here is the *real* presence.

B: Is this a quantitative or qualitative distinction?

S: Qualitative.

B: What is this quality? For me the sacraments have power to testify. Our action as such in the Lord's Supper cannot *give* the immediate relation. The Lord Himself can create this presence. Sacraments are *means* to this relation, but 'means' denotes 'witness'. What man can do can only be a witness.

S: You place preaching alongside the two sacraments of Baptism and the Lord's Supper. Is there no difference?

B: The difference is one of means. Certainly Baptism and the Lord's Supper concern those who *belong* to the Church. Baptism and the Lord's Supper are speaking or signifying actions, but I see no real difference. I would prefer to abrogate the word 'sacrament' or to use 'sacrament' for all ecclesiastical actions. All are 'signs'.

S: Why preserve Baptism and the Lord's Supper in the Church?

B: These are commanded by our Lord. We need these signs together with the sign of the Word. They remind us that the Word of God is not just something said, but is a *deed*. The essence of the Lord's Supper is that we eat together: an *action*.

S: Should footwashing be placed on the same level?

86

B: This shows us the relativity of the whole question.

S: What is the relation between Baptism and faith?

B: In the New Testament the two cannot be separated. The man who is baptised *really* performs an *action* of faith. Why does a man ask to be baptised? He is asking for a confirmation of his faith. The community baptises him, and he accomplishes this act of confession. He will not be alone with his faith, but will be with the community. Baptism is a confirmation, not a cause, of faith. It gives certainty. The acting subject in Baptism is the Lord Himself.

S: What is the objection to water as a 'causative means' in Baptism?

B: If Jesus Christ is the Baptiser, then what the minister does can only be as a representative of Christ. No *causae secundae*! We need no repetition or realisation of our redemption. Christ has achieved all of this perfectly, once-for-all! The task of the Church is to announce the good news of the perfect work of Christ done for all. Salvation is complete. There is no need for supplementation.

S: You claim that Baptism has not a causative or regenerative, but a *cognitive* aim. Do you base this 'cognitive' interpretation on New Testament texts?

B: No, this is a later question. I do not insist on the word 'cognitive'. What concerns me is that salvation be not limited. Sacraments are not means for the gift of grace, but means of the *announcement* of the gift of grace. The fulness of salvation must not be limited by the deeds of ministers and the Church. The Church is a witnessing Church, and that is not a small thing! It is even too much! Paul was living in the first century, before Catholicism and the misinterpretation of Romans 6. He could be strong in *realistic* affirmation; there was no need for negative hedging as I do.

S: Was the entire race redeemed at Golgotha?

B: The distinction is not between redeemed and non-redeemed, but between those who realise it and those who do not. The emphasis in much of today's preaching has to do with salvation in the future, something the preacher can help give, instead of speaking of the perfect salvation already accomplished. We only await its final revelation. The emphasis should be on the deed of God that is *done*. *Cognitio* means the *gnosis* of the *pistis*. Faith is a form of knowledge. Thus out of faith comes confession. Confession is the expression of the knowledge of faith.

S: How does the Church guard against anti-sacramentalists?

B: By obeying the command of Christ. The command of Jesus Christ is a command of wisdom. He knows the relation between Word and deed. Anti-sacramentalists are spiritualists who do not understand the realism of the faith. Something *externally happened* in the world, and this is the basis of faith, not something that is only told.

Session 2: Sections IV and V

S: Is the cognitive understanding of Baptism really adequate?

B: Yes. Knowledge is something *real*. Christian knowledge is in itself full of communion with reality as such. One knows and one is made to know—both. Baptism is a witness given by the Lord of the Church to a member in which He makes him know something special about his knowledge, makes sure the member's knowledge. I am made a Christian because a Christian, unlike others, *knows something*. It is this that makes a Christian: his knowing about Christ. The Christian receives an assurance and testimony in Baptism. He is not an isolated believer, for he receives an answer: 'Your faith is accepted and good.'

S: Does not your view overemphasise subjectivism and individualism?

B: I? I am accused of such things! Explain yourself.

S: You do not stress antecedent grace.

B: Poor Church, that knows only antecedent grace in Baptism! There is confusion in the Church. Instead of looking at Christ as the fountain of grace and power, the Church has invented the doctrine of the sacraments: objectivity in what the Church is doing. Christ is practically shoved into the background! Divine objectivity rests in the Church's action now. Confusion! Sacramentalism is a pseudo-objectivism. Completely false!

S: Does not the cognitive understanding overemphasise correctness of doctrine? Who must have the orthodox doctrine, the baptised or the Church?

B: I cannot understand your introducing the question of orthodox doctrine. Where does it come in?

S: On page 39 you talk of 'professing a faith quite other than

88

that of the New Testament', and so on. Yet you have emphasised that man can do nothing, that nothing can effect the working of Christ in Baptism. You speak of 'false Church', 'light' and 'darkness', etc.

B: Baptism is in danger in a false Church, but my point is this: notwithstanding the weakness of faith, Baptism has its cognitive power. The purity of the Church is no condition for the power of Baptism. Baptism is Baptism even if I have serious objections to the baptising Church. Here comes a question of order: where is the true faith? Our faith is a mixture of right and wrong!

S: In the cognitive view it does depend on the knowledge of the Church.

B: No, knowledge of Christ the Lord. Here the question of orthodoxy and heterodoxy is not important. Baptism is endangered in a bad Church, so we are obliged to do our best.

S: If Baptism is merely a sign, why did Jesus command it? What is the relation of what Jesus commands to the *ordering* of Baptism?

B: I object to the word 'merely'. Baptism is a *sign* asked for and given by the same Lord who has done what He has done. He has called a community as such, and this and that man. Perhaps we should say 'picture' instead of 'sign'. Baptism is a picture of what Christ did and what He is: the crucified and risen Lord. Our justification and sanctification lie hidden in heaven. This picture cannot be belittled. If Christ has put man in this picture, then it is no small thing. As to why Jesus commanded it, ask Him. There is only one place in the New Testament where we have the literal expression of this command: Matthew 28. But perhaps a stronger form of this command is Jesus' own baptism by John. If we have to follow Him, then why not understand our life as beginning with what He did? Even without Matthew 28, the story of Jesus' baptism is strong enough to express the will of the Lord. A Christian life begins as His. We have to enter this picture. The picture is just a picture, not the real death and resurrection. But in this picture we see what will come to us.

S: Then Baptism must be indispensable.

B: I do not oppose that. One must obey the command. But remember: the picture is not the *reality*, and the reality may replace the picture! Remember what I said at the first of the monograph about this. The form of how we enter into this picture *may* be different. The command is not a *law*, not a paragraph out of a law book. We obey out of respect, but if there are hindrances, there is no reason to despair or to condemn someone. In his early years Luther liked to speak of 'spiritual baptism'. He did not continue to speak so, but maybe he was right. We cannot always preach, either. A great part of our lives is not spent in preaching, notwithstanding the fact that we are commanded to preach.

S: What about the use of incorrect order? Does this annul the power of Baptism?

B: Even an imperfect order is an order. Maybe the order can be changed. Immersing was usual in New Testament times, and we have changed the order; but this implies no loss of the effect of Baptism. *He* is strong even if we are weak!

S: In Romans 6.3-4, Paul says: 'Do you not know that all of us who have been baptised into Christ Jesus were baptised into his death? We were buried therefore with him by baptism into death, so that as Christ was raised from the dead by the glory of the Father, we too might walk in newness of life.' Exegesis please! Does verse 3 imply a general baptism of all at the Cross?

B: No. Baptised *in* Him, *in His death*. What does this mean? Paul continues: we were buried with Him by baptism in His death, etc. If we are 'in the picture', that is, put into the picture of His death, we have the promise that we will be in His resurrection.

S: According to the Greek, we are baptised *into* Christ, not *in* Christ. There is an objective change, not just a sign. Our condition is altered.

B: The question is: What does the Greek word translated 'to baptise' mean? It means that we join in the *picture*, and the picture is of Christ's death. We are put in relation to Christ, receiving this participation in the picture of His death.

S: Are we not baptised into His death, rather than into the picture? Is there not an ontological change?

B: Yes, a *real* change. We are persons who *know* this. In this *knowledge* I enter into this relation. This is not 'merely' knowledge, because the knowledge given is the Holy Spirit's knowledge. For me the noetic and the ontological are *one* here.

S: Where do you find the cognitive in Romans 6?

B: *Homoiōma* in verse 5 is the point for me. The picture! Look at the context. Paul has asked at the beginning: May we sin in order to magnify grace? His answer: No! Because the old man dies with Christ (united with Him in a death *like His*) and sin is no longer there. Baptism is the sign of this.

S: Is not the likeness (*homoiōma*) more *concrete* than a picture? Is not this a *real* likeness?

B: Baptism is a parable of the Kingdom, and parables are good in the New Testament. I think verse 3 must be interpreted in terms of verse 5.

S: If you do not agree with the practice of infant baptism, then what age do you consider a person ready for Baptism: twelve to sixteen years?

B: For me baptism is not a question of age. A mere child may be so advanced in faith and the Christian life that I might take the responsibility of baptising him. I had an experience like this about thirty years ago in Göttingen. A Jewish boy of nine read the New Testament (from a 'Children's Bible') in school, and he told his parents that he believed that the New Testament is the correct completion of the Old, and that he wanted to be baptised. His father came to me and asked what he should do. We arranged for me to talk with the boy, and I was convinced that he knew what he was doing. So I baptised him! What counts with me is this: first, that somebody (child or adult) *wishes* to be baptised and *asks*; second, that when I ask: 'Why do you wish it?' he can explain his reason for wanting Baptism. If he can, then I will do it. Conversion cannot be known or tested. Merely the wish to be baptised is enough, and a small but serious confession of faith should go *before* Baptism, not something afterwards like Confirmation!

S: In the context of Baptism you identify the noetic and the ontological, and you admit that there is an ontological difference between the baptised and the unbaptised. Yet earlier this year, speaking in connexion with the missionary endeavour of the Church, you stressed that there was no ontological difference between the Christian and the non-Christian. How do you reconcile this seeming contradiction?

B: The saving work of Jesus Christ is the same for all men. That Christ died for all provides a common ontological basis for *all* men. However, we must remember that ontology is not something static and fixed. Within this ontological structure that is valid for all, there are ontological differences. When a man has faith and is baptised, then he *knows* (noetic) something that changes his life (ontic). This *knowledge* is *reality*, so that the baptised man does undergo an ontological (noetic) change within the once-for-all ontological condition created for all men by Jesus Christ.

S: In relation to infant baptism, what about the baptism of whole households in the New Testament?

B: It always stresses in these cases that at least *one* member of the household *has faith*, and it does not mention children.

D. *The Christian Understanding of Revelation**

Session 1: Sections 1-4

S: Under point 1 on page 207 (*Against the Stream*) you speak of Christian revelation as one that decides man's being or non-being. What is one if he does not accept revelation?

B: A small, but important misunderstanding! Your question is based on the presupposition that revelation is thrust upon man and that he *must* accept. I did not intend to describe revelation as such a thing. I tried to give a description of revelation that is not accidental but *necessary* news for man. Without it he is in *nihil*, death, nonbeing. 'Must' does not refer to physical constraint, but means that it is objectively necessary to be accepted if man is to escape death. This is not so, for instance, in a scientific revelation. Christian revelation is indispensable. That is the way I understand Paul's preaching to the Athenians. This text means: the Judge of the world is revealed. Thus this is a question of being or nonbeing, life or death. Does the man who refuses revelation cease to be a man? No, for judgment is not yet executed. Judgment means death. A dead man is a corpse. He has ceased to be man. There is no objective possibility of refusing to hear revelation. A subjective possibility, yes. But revelation is not something to be taken or refused. Man's rejection is not normal, but abnormal. The man who rejects revelation is in the state of sin, which means rebellion against his created nature.

S: Under point 3 you state that Christian revelation is always

---

* The title of Stanley Godman's English translation of *Das christliche Verständnis der Offenbarung, Theologische Existenz heute*, Neue Folge, Heft 12, 1948. Published in *Against the Stream*, The S.C.M. Press, London, 1954.

completely new to man: yesterday, today, and tomorrow. Is revelation continually full of surprises? Is there no constancy, no continuity of revelation? God's sun, which rises every morning, has continuity of creational rhythm. Can we not expect the same continuity in God's revelation? Do we not have in the Ten Commandments a revelation of God's will that will never change?

B: We are not in possession of *general* information about the will of God. God must give us the true interpretation of His commandments. God will never command us to lie; if *He* commands us, we are not lying, even if our hearing and obeying in this case seem contradictory to some moral standards to which we are accustomed. You say, 'The sun which rises every morning has continuity of creational rhythm.' I accept your parable. Now you ask if revelation has such a continuity. The light and warmth of the sun is always new. A new day is an event to be *hoped* for. Jesus speaks of the night when there can be no more work. The day, the revelation, is a gift. We cannot capitalise it. The continuity lies in God's trustworthiness, Jesus Christ. I do not like the word 'surprise' in this connexion. The point is: grace is not to be foreseen, but will always be totally new as a gift from God, an address from God in His Word. We are concerned here not with a natural sequence of events, but with God as a Person (not an institution or scientific automaton) who gives us His grace. The continuity of revelation comes from above. The question of 'being in Christ' is a question to be answered always anew. And what you are is a *new* creature. Christ is the *same*, but as the same He is for me who lives in time always a new mystery, a new miracle. 'New' is not chiefly a temporal description, but a spiritual condition. We are always in the beginning, and this is not a bad, but a good thing. 'The mercy of God is every morning new.'

S: Under point 4 you state that the Christian revelation is intended 'for all men'. Can this be said of the Old Testament revelation? Was revelation *general* revelation *before* the incarnation? If the Old Testament Jews had the Messianic vocation, what does the incarnation mean? If the revelation in Christ was for all, then why does John emphasise that Jesus first came to 'his own' (John 1.11), who received Him not, and why does Paul emphasise that the Gentiles are given the revelation only after the Jews have rejected it (Romans 11.11-24)? Do you propound in the *Church Dogmatics* a developing (not just un-folding) *Heilsgeschichte* (history of salvation)?

B: There are serious revelations that are not meant for all men, but the Word of God is for all. This is not accidental, but so that no man can excuse himself by saying, 'Revelation is not for me.' The revelation in the Old Testament was for all men. The Hebrews were destined to be messengers to the whole world. This may be hidden in some parts, but not in Isaiah. The incarnation means that the history of Israel had come to its end. There is but one revelation, and the step from the Old Testament to the New is the *Heilsgeschichte*. Promise is fulfilled. One could say that the relation between promise and fulfilment is the *Heilsgeschichte*. As for the Jews, they remain God's chosen people (Romans 9-11). God does not change things. The Jews remain chosen people even if they reject Christ! The Gentiles are grafted in after the incarnation, and yet revelation was meant for the Gentiles from the beginning. Now for your question about *Heilsgeschichte*. Yes, I have a *Heilsgeschichte*—at least, I hope so. The decree of God is unfolding, but in a developing series of acts. *Heilsgeschichte* is both unfolding and developing.

S: This is another question about your assertion that revelation is 'for all men'. In Romans 3.23-24 Paul says that since all have sinned and fall short of the glory of God, they are justified by his grace as a gift. But have you forgotten Paul's quali-fication in the previous verse (3.22), that this justification is 'for all *who believe*'?

B: Christ's justification is perfect. John says that Christ died not only for us, but for the whole world. Reconciliation is per-fect, and reconciliation means for me both justification and sanctification. From God's side everything necessary has been done for all men. This must be announced. The 'for' in the phrase 'for all who believe' (Greek: *'eis'* in *'eis pantas tous pisteuontas'*) is looking forward; the good news must be accepted by faith. Paul had to announce the Gospel all over the Medi-terranean world, for people did not yet know about the good news. He will go to spread faith: *eis pantas*. *Pistis* (faith) can only look back upon what has become true. The Apostle can only cry out: 'Believe!'—not in his faith, but in Christ. I have a suspicion that there is a hidden Pelagianism in the Anglo-Saxon mind! This shows up in your question. But the truth is that the relation between the objective reality of reconciliation and subjective affirmation is a gift of the Holy Spirit.

S: On page 211 you say that 'there is no room for revelation in the Christian sense in any human inquiry or any human faculty of reason'. Does this mean that the *Church Dogmatics* itself is 'baptised philosophy'?

B: There is no theory which as such has room for revelation, no room as if man could provide room for revelation; but revelation can make room for itself. When revelation is present in the midst of a human theory (whether theology or philosophy), that is a miracle, comparable with the Virgin Birth! You ask if the *Church Dogmatics* is a 'baptised philosophy'? 'Baptised', not 'born'! That means a new start! I do not make room for revelation. I reflect upon it; I do my best. But when revelation happens in a human endeavour, God is at work, not the minister or even a professor! Theology can only be done in a constant act of prayer. It must be a kind of adoration. God is not bound to confess Himself to an act of man. It is a serious thing when a minister prays at the beginning of a worship service and invokes God's presence. It is the same in theology. We have to pray, and then we have to believe that God is now present. If I do not believe it, I cannot work in certainty and serenity. One has to pray to be in God's service. Then my language is resolute, not from my own assurance, but from God.

S: It is the same for a philosopher.

B: Philosophers will be in heaven also! But I cannot put myself in the place of a philosopher.

S: Did not Calvin believe in an innate knowledge of God in man, an *innata religio*?

B: The chapter at the beginning of the *Institutes*, where Calvin speaks of this, is not clear. I am not sure that Calvin is not near some kind of natural disposition. I do not think this danger has had bad consequences in his *Institutes*, but he set a bad example. Twenty years after his death natural theology appeared in Reformed theology. But in Calvin this religious condition was not meant as preparation. In the Fall this natural religious inclination has become man's worst enemy! It produces all forms of idolatry. So in Calvin there is no way from *innata religio* to the acceptance of the Gospel. We should hate this word 'religion'! Christianity is not a religion. It is not one kind of a general religion. Let us extinguish this use of the word.

'Religion' is a characteristic of humanity, but faith does not grow out of it, even if Calvin has supposed such a thing as *religio innata*!

Session 2: Sections 5-8

S: Does this section represent an *analogia relationis* to the Trinity, that is, revelation to *man* by the *Bible* through the *Church*?

B: No. An analogy would be Incarnation, Bible, Church.

S: Is the *imago Dei* (man-woman relation) an *analogia relationis* to the Trinity?

B: Yes, insofar as the man-woman relation (*imago Dei*) is a human togetherness, the fundamental form of human co-existence. This *imago Dei* may be said to be an analogy to the Trinity insofar as there is in God a togetherness. But in the *imago Dei* there is no Trinity. The *tertium comparationis* would be the 'togetherness'. But I would prefer to explain the *imago Dei* in Genesis 1 as a picture of God in relation to Israel. This relation is a kind of marriage. This is a prefiguring of how God acts with His people and is later continued in the relation between Jesus Christ and the Church.

S: Can the Holy Spirit speak only through the Bible?

B: No. The Holy Spirit has not retired. Calvin insisted on the omnipresence of the Holy Spirit. But if we must distinguish between the Holy Spirit and other spirits, then the Bible is the criterion.

S: What is the merit of being a *direct* witness, like the prophets and apostles?

B: There is no merit, but a distinction. The prophets and apostles have participated in the history of the true revelation. We have only a mediated witness. Prophets were not only direct witnesses, but *participated* in the history, and so did the apostles. The Old Testament is not only a witness to the deed of God, but of God's working with the prophets. It is the same in the New Testament. It not only is a witness to Christ, but also to those in His Body. Augustine, Luther, and we base our faith on the witness of these men. It is not because of merit, but because of the *fact* that they, and not we, were with Christ.

S: What is the difference between the prophets and later Church figures, e.g. Augustine?

B: The prophets of the Old Testament give testimony to the

covenant made in the realm of this people, a covenant that has a goal or future not yet accomplished.

S: Is there *Heilsgeschichte* in the Old Testament?

B: Yes, the first step. Israel fails to keep the covenant, but God remains faithful. In Christ He takes the role of man and fulfils the covenant Himself, once-for-all. The prophets are witnesses to the covenant and to this extent are prophets of Jesus Christ within Israel, and the people of Israel is the presence of Christ insofar as He is there *in promise*.

S: On what grounds can we criticise or attack the interpretation of Holy Scripture by others in which they claim the guidance of the Holy Spirit? For instance, if someone said we should accept footwashing, on what grounds could we accept or reject it?

B: I do not think we have to reject footwashing. The question is one of meaning. Sound exegesis is the criterion.

S: What if two people differ on interpretation?

B: In every century the Church has had to find out anew the meaning of Scripture. The task remains. We must trust that the Holy Spirit will lead us into all truth. We have no pope in Protestantism, but we do have *secondary* criteria. Sound exegesis will be done *within the communion of saints*. The Bible is given to the community of the Church. Tradition helps us toward sound exegesis, and tradition includes the whole history of the Church (including the nineteenth century!). Confessions also help, but none of these is an absolute criterion. In interpretation, tradition and Church Fathers and confessions are our 'parents' whom we must respect and honour, but there are times when a breach must be made (Reformation!).

S: Where is the right tradition? What church has it?

B: We cannot say. No one church has all the truth. Each church should understand itself only as a *means*. Churches are bound to go their own way as they see it. Insofar as a church has Jesus Christ it has God the Truth. Churches participate in the Truth, but the Truth is only Jesus Christ. Jesus Christ interprets Himself in the Church. He churches us; we cannot be our own churches. At the end-time we will probably all be astonished! What we have in our hands is relative, but we are in the hands of the eternal Truth of God.

S: Does each church have a piece of the Truth or the whole Truth?

B: Insofar as Jesus Christ is there, the Church has the whole Truth. But in another sense it must be said that each has a part, for there are dissensions.

S: But Truth cannot be broken.

B: In the mirror of our Christian concepts it is broken, but not in Christ. If we look to Christ, He is the one and whole Truth. I am a Reformed churchman and would not be a Lutheran or Roman or Orthodox, but I would never say that the Reformed Church has the whole truth!

S: Paul Tillich criticises your use of 'kerygmatic'. The Bible is written in words that have a philosophical history and meaning. If we use these words, are we not forced into a philosophical school? Can we be kerygmatic and not apologetic?

B: I am trying to understand your question. Are not even prophets and apostles in philosophy because they use words? It is true that we cannot escape words, and words bring us into the realm of philosophy. But the question is whether the intention of the prophets and apostles is to spread a certain manner of thought, a system, a *Weltanschauung*. Are we as interpreters interested in a *Weltanschauung*? Let us begin with the Bible! I do not think the prophets and apostles were interested in philosophy, but they used words to give an account of what happened to them. Now if we understand them, we have to understand their words, but our interest is not to promulgate a philosophy, but to look where they were looking. The crucial point is *where the interest lies*. Their interest did not lie in philosophy, but in using words to point to revelation. The task of theology cannot be to form another religious philosophy. Tillich has not yet become a theologian. He remains in the realm of the philosophical attempt. Theology begins where the philosophical attempt ends, notwithstanding the fact that we are using philosophical terms.

S: Can a church ever *cease* being the Church?

B: Looking on human beings who are the constituents of a church, a church cannot only cease to be the Church, but it must. We as human beings are not able to uphold the real Church. The church as a human work is a *lost* work. 'Without me you can do nothing,' said Jesus. But in Matthew 16.18 Jesus says to Peter, 'On you I will build my Church.' That is His promise. The Church is upheld by the Lord and lives on promise. Every church lives on the edge of the abyss. If it is living, it is by the grace of the Lord. For myself, I would never say that any church ceases to be Church. The Lord does not forsake His Church, but we can only hold on to His promise. Looking at us, I say the Church must cease; looking at Him, I say the Church will always be preserved. Christian faith must be strong not only for the individual, but for the Church. This is necessary in order to be able to preach and work in the Church. I do not like Quaker practices, but I would not say they were not Church.

S: Are there two concepts of freedom: 'free will' and 'freedom for'?

B: I would prefer to differentiate between a true and a false freedom. True freedom is not a choice between alternatives; our one freedom is obedience to the will of God. What we call freedom as 'free will' is not freedom. We are free if we agree with God, otherwise we are prisoners.

S: Can we choose freedom? Have we the ability?

B: The liberty of free will is sin! It is the shame of humanity that we live as if we could choose.

APPENDIX: AN OUTLINE OF KARL BARTH'S *CHURCH DOGMATICS*

VOL. I: WORD OF GOD

Part 1

Introduction

1. The Task of Dogmatics
2. The Task of Prolegomena to Dogmatics

Ch. 1 *The Word of God as the Criterion of Dogmatics*

3. Church Proclamation as the Material of Dogmatics
4. The Word of God in Its Threefold Form
5. The Nature of the Word of God
6. The Knowability of the Word of God
7. The Word of God, Dogma, and Dogmatics

Ch. 2 *The Revelation of God*

Sect. 1. The Triune God
8. God in His Revelation
9. God's Three-in-Oneness
10. God the Father
11. God the Son
12. God the Holy Spirit

Part 2

Sect. 2. The Incarnation of the Word
13. God's Freedom for Man

VOL. II: GOD

Part 1

Ch. 5 *The Knowledge of God*

25. The Fulfilment of the Knowledge of God
26. The Knowability of God
27. The Limits of the Knowledge of God

Ch. 6 *The Reality of God*

28. The Being of God as the One Who Loves in Freedom
29. The Perfections of God
30. The Perfections of the Divine Loving
31. The Perfections of the Divine Freedom

Part 2

Ch. 7 *The Election of God*

32. The Problem of a Correct Doctrine of the Election of Grace
33. The Election of Jesus Christ
34. The Election of the Community
35. The Election of the Individual

Ch. 8 *The Command of God*

36. Ethics as a Task of the Doctrine of God

VOL. III: CREATION

Part 1

Ch. 9 *The Work of Creation*

40. Faith in God the Creator
41. Creation and Covenant
42. The Yes of God the Creator

Part 2

Ch. 10 *The Creature*

43. Man as a Problem of Dogmatics
44. Man as the Creature of God
45. Man in His Determination as the Covenant-Partner of God
46. Man as Soul and Body
47. Man in His Time

Part 3

Ch. 11 *The Creator and His Creature*

48. The Doctrine of Providence, its Basis and Form
49. God the Father as Lord of His Creature
50. God and Nothingness
51. The Kingdom of Heaven, the Ambassadors of God and their Opponents

VOL. IV: RECONCILIATION

Part 1

Ch. 13 *The Subject-matter and Problems of the Doctrine of Reconciliation*

57. The Work of God the Reconciler
58. The Doctrine of Reconciliation (Survey)

Ch. 14 *Jesus Christ, the Lord as Servant*

59. The Obedience of the Son of God
60. The Pride and Fall of Man
61. The Justification of Man
62. The Holy Spirit and the Gathering of the Christian Community
63. The Holy Spirit and Christian Faith

Part 2

Ch. 15 *Jesus Christ, the Servant as Lord*

64. The Exaltation of the Son of Man
65. The Sloth and Misery of Man
66. The Sanctification of Man

VOL. V: REDEMPTION

WORD OF GOD

14. The Time of Revelation
15. The Secret of Revelation

Sect. 3. The Outpouring of the Holy Spirit

16. The Freedom of Man for God
17. God's Revelation as the Abolition of Religion
18. The Life of the Children of God

Ch. 3 *Holy Scripture*

19. The Word of God for the Church
20. Authority in the Church
21. Freedom in the Church

Ch. 4 *The Proclamation of the Church*

22. The Mission of the Church
23. Dogmatics as a Function of the Hearing Church
24. Dogmatics as a Function of the Teaching Church

GOD

37. The Command as the Claim of God
38. The Command as the Decision of God
39. The Command as the Judgment of God

CREATION

Part 4

Ch. 12 *The Command of God the Creator*

52. Ethics as a Task of the Doctrine of Creation
53. Freedom Before God
54. Freedom in Fellowship
55. Freedom for Life
56. Freedom in Limitation

RECONCILIATION

67. The Holy Spirit and the Upbuilding of the Christian Community
68. The Holy Spirit and Christian Love

Part 3

Ch. 16 *Jesus Christ, the True Witness*

69. The Glory of the Mediator
70. The Falsehood and Condemnation of Man
71. The Vocation of Man
72. The Holy Spirit and the Sending of the Christian Community
73. The Holy Spirit and Christian Hope

Part 4

Ch. 17 *The Command of God the Reconciler*

REDEMPTION